First World War
and Army of Occupation
War Diary
France, Belgium and Germany

39 DIVISION
117 Infantry Brigade,
Brigade Machine Gun Company
and Brigade Trench Mortar Battery
16 May 1916 - 28 February 1918

WO95/2587/4-5

The Naval & Military Press Ltd
www.nmarchive.com
Published in association with The National Archives

Published by

The Naval & Military Press Ltd

Unit 10 Ridgewood Industrial Park,

Uckfield, East Sussex,

TN22 5QE England

Tel: +44 (0) 1825 749494

www.naval-military-press.com

www.nmarchive.com

This diary has been reprinted in facsimile from the original. Any imperfections are inevitably reproduced and the quality may fall short of modern type and cartographic standards.

Contents

Document type	Place/Title	Date From	Date To
Heading	WO95/2587/4		
Heading	117th Machine Gun Coy. May 1916-Feb 1918		
Heading	117th Brigade Machine Gun Coy. May 1916		
War Diary	Havre	16/05/1916	16/05/1916
War Diary	Le Hamel (Bethune)	18/05/1916	28/05/1916
Heading	117th Brigade Machine Gun Company June 1916		
Miscellaneous	D.A.G. 3rd Ech.	30/06/1916	30/06/1916
War Diary	Givenchy	01/06/1916	05/06/1916
War Diary	Ferme Du Roi	07/06/1916	07/06/1916
War Diary	Le Hamel	10/06/1916	10/06/1916
War Diary	Loisne	17/06/1916	30/06/1916
Miscellaneous	Headquarters 39th Division	05/06/1916	05/06/1916
Heading	117th Brigade Machine Gun Company. July 1916		
Miscellaneous	Headquarters 117th Brigade		
War Diary	Loisne	11/07/1916	14/07/1916
War Diary	Le Touret	16/07/1916	21/07/1916
War Diary	La Couture	21/07/1916	21/07/1916
War Diary	Le Hamel	25/07/1916	25/07/1916
War Diary	Givenchy	27/07/1916	31/07/1916
Heading	117th Brigade Machine Gun Company August 1916		
War Diary	Givenchy	01/08/1916	05/08/1916
War Diary	Bethune	06/08/1916	09/08/1916
War Diary	Auchel	10/08/1916	10/08/1916
War Diary	Rocourt	11/08/1916	11/08/1916
War Diary	Orlencourt	12/08/1916	22/08/1916
War Diary	Maisnil-St-Pol	23/08/1916	23/08/1916
War Diary	La Closerie Fm	24/08/1916	24/08/1916
War Diary	Vauchelles	25/08/1916	27/08/1916
War Diary	Bertrancourt	28/08/1916	31/08/1916
Heading	117th Brigade Machine Gun Company September 1916		
War Diary	Bertrancourt	01/09/1916	05/09/1916
War Diary	Mailly-Maillet	06/09/1916	20/09/1916
War Diary	Courcelle-Au-Bois	20/09/1916	21/09/1916
War Diary	Courcelle	21/09/1916	30/09/1916
Heading	117th Brigade Machine Gun Company October 1916		
War Diary	Courcelle	01/10/1916	01/10/1916
War Diary	Bertrancourt Martinsart	02/10/1916	02/10/1916
War Diary	Martinsart	03/10/1916	04/10/1916
War Diary	Thiepval	05/10/1916	10/10/1916
War Diary	Martinsart	14/10/1916	16/10/1916
War Diary	Authville	17/10/1916	26/10/1916
War Diary	Pioneer Rd	27/10/1916	27/10/1916
War Diary	Authville	28/10/1916	29/10/1916
War Diary	Senlis	30/10/1916	31/10/1916
Heading	117th Brigade Machine Gun Company November 1916		
War Diary	Senlis	01/11/1916	03/11/1916
War Diary	Authville	04/11/1916	05/11/1916
War Diary	Senlis	06/11/1916	06/11/1916
War Diary	Authville	07/11/1916	08/11/1916
War Diary	Pioneer Road	09/11/1916	11/11/1916

War Diary	Senlis	12/11/1916	12/11/1916
War Diary	Authville	13/11/1916	14/11/1916
War Diary	Warloy	15/11/1916	15/11/1916
War Diary	Beauval	16/11/1916	18/11/1916
War Diary	Bellezeele	19/11/1916	30/11/1916
Operation(al) Order(s)	Operation Order No. 5 By Captain A Hall Commanding 117 M G Coy		
Operation(al) Order(s)	Operation Order No. 8 By Captain A Hall Commanding 117 M G Coy		
Operation(al) Order(s)	117th Infantry Brigade Order No. 89	31/10/1916	31/10/1916
Heading	117th Brigade Machine Gun Company December 1916		
War Diary	Bollezeele	01/12/1916	10/12/1916
War Diary	Herzeele	11/12/1916	11/12/1916
War Diary	Poperinghe	12/12/1916	12/12/1916
War Diary	Ypres	12/12/1916	31/12/1916
Operation(al) Order(s)	117th Infantry Brigade Order No. 103	05/12/1916	05/12/1916
Miscellaneous	March Table to accompany 117th Infantry Brigade Order No. 103		
Miscellaneous	117th Infantry Brigade Order No. 104	06/12/1916	06/12/1916
Miscellaneous	Programme For Inspection Of 117th Infantry Brigade by Lieut. General Sir Aylmer Hunter-Weston, K.C.B., D.S.O., Commanding VIII Corps	08/12/1916	08/12/1916
Diagram etc	Ceremonial		
Miscellaneous	117th Infantry Brigade Order No. 105	09/12/1916	09/12/1916
Miscellaneous	Table "A" to accompany 117th Infantry Brigade Order No. 105		
Miscellaneous			
Miscellaneous	Table "B" to accompany 117th Infantry Brigade Order No. 104		
Miscellaneous	Amendment To 117th Infantry Brigade Order No. 105	10/12/1916	10/12/1916
Miscellaneous	Further Amendments To 117th Infantry Brigade Order No. 105	10/12/1916	10/12/1916
Operation(al) Order(s)	117th Infantry Brigade Order No. 106	11/12/1916	11/12/1916
Miscellaneous	Relief Table to accompany 117th Infantry Brigade Order No. 106		
Miscellaneous	Disposition Table To Accompany 117th Infantry Brigade Order No. 106		
War Diary	Ypres	02/01/1917	16/01/1917
War Diary	Brandhoek	17/01/1917	24/01/1917
War Diary	Wieltje	25/01/1917	31/01/1917
Miscellaneous	117th Infantry Brigade Order No. 116	10/01/1917	10/01/1917
Miscellaneous	Relief Table To Accompany 117th Infantry Brigade Order No. 116		
Miscellaneous	Amendment To 117th Infantry Brigade Order No. 116	11/01/1917	11/01/1917
War Diary	Weltje	01/02/1917	03/02/1917
War Diary	Railway Wood	04/02/1917	18/02/1917
War Diary	S Camp	19/02/1917	25/02/1917
War Diary	Ypres	26/02/1917	28/02/1917
Operation(al) Order(s)	117 M.G.Co. Operation Order No. 20	10/02/1917	10/02/1917
Miscellaneous	Table Of Gun Position & Targets		
Miscellaneous	Amendment To 117 M.G.Co. Order No. 20	11/02/1917	11/02/1917
Miscellaneous	117th Infantry Brigade Order No. 127	14/02/1917	14/02/1917
Miscellaneous	Relief Table to accompany 117th Infantry Brigade Order No. 127		
Miscellaneous	Location And Work Table		
Miscellaneous	117th Infantry Brigade Order No. 124	09/02/1917	09/02/1917

Miscellaneous	Table "A" Raid Barrage (18 Ponder)		
Miscellaneous	Table "B" Action Of Machine Guns.		
Miscellaneous	Amendment To 117th Infantry Brigade Order No. 124	11/02/1917	11/02/1917
Miscellaneous	Table "D"		
Miscellaneous	Second Amendment To 117th Infantry Brigade Order No. 124	12/02/1917	12/02/1917
War Diary	Ypres	01/03/1917	09/03/1917
War Diary	Erie Camp	10/03/1917	15/03/1917
War Diary	Ypres	16/03/1917	26/03/1917
War Diary	Erie Camp	27/03/1917	01/04/1917
War Diary	Ypres	02/04/1917	10/04/1917
War Diary	Erie Camp	11/04/1917	13/04/1917
War Diary	Merckeghem	14/04/1917	27/04/1917
War Diary	Z Camp	28/04/1917	30/04/1917
War Diary	S Camp	01/05/1917	16/05/1917
War Diary	Hill Top Sector	16/05/1917	31/05/1917
War Diary	D Camp	01/06/1917	07/06/1917
War Diary	S Camp	08/06/1917	14/06/1917
War Diary	Hill Top Sector	15/06/1917	30/06/1917
War Diary	C Camp	01/07/1917	01/07/1917
War Diary	Salperwick	02/07/1917	21/07/1917
War Diary	A 30 Camp	22/07/1917	29/07/1917
War Diary	Hill Top Sector	30/07/1917	05/08/1917
War Diary	War Diary 117 Coy M.G.C. 1st Jan-31 Jan 1918 (inclusive)		
War Diary	Meteren	06/08/1917	13/08/1917
War Diary	Ridge Wood	14/08/1917	15/08/1917
War Diary	Bluff Tunnels	16/08/1917	19/08/1917
War Diary	Ridge Wood	20/08/1917	22/08/1917
War Diary	Hollebeke	23/08/1917	28/08/1917
War Diary	Murrumbidgee Camp	29/08/1917	31/08/1917
Operation(al) Order(s)	Operation Order By Capt. H.M. Pasteur Commdg 117 M.G. Coy	14/08/1917	14/08/1917
Operation(al) Order(s)	Operation Orders No. 8 By Capt. F.M. Pasteur Comdg 117th Machine Gun Company.		
Heading	War Diary 1 Sept-30 Sept 1917 (inclusive) 117 Coy Machine Gun Corps.		
War Diary	Murrumbidgee Camp	01/09/1917	10/09/1917
War Diary	Ridge Camp	11/09/1917	12/09/1917
War Diary	Larch Wood	13/09/1917	14/09/1917
War Diary	Ridge Wood	15/09/1917	15/09/1917
War Diary	Millekruisse Area	16/09/1917	19/09/1917
War Diary	The Ravine & Bulgar Wood)	20/09/1917	21/09/1917
War Diary	Ridge Wood	26/09/1917	26/09/1917
War Diary	Clonnel Copse	27/09/1917	28/09/1917
War Diary	Locre	29/09/1917	30/09/1917
War Diary	Ridge Wood	21/09/1917	21/09/1917
War Diary	Ascot Camp Westoutre	22/09/1917	24/09/1917
War Diary	Ridge Wood	25/09/1917	25/09/1917
War Diary	Locre	01/10/1917	15/10/1917
War Diary	Willebeek Camp N 9.d 7.5.	16/10/1917	19/10/1917
War Diary	Shrewsbury Forest Sector	20/10/1917	24/10/1917
War Diary	Willebeek Camp	24/10/1917	29/10/1917
War Diary	Camp Near Brasserie At N 5.d 9.9	30/10/1917	31/10/1917
Operation(al) Order(s)	Operation Order No. 6 By Capt L.E.H. Whitby Commanding 117th Machine Gun Company.	15/10/1917	15/10/1917

Operation(al) Order(s)	Operation Order No. 7 By Capt L.E.H. Whitby	19/10/1917	19/10/1917
Operation(al) Order(s)	Operation Order No. 8 By Capt L.E.H. Whitby		
War Diary	Ypres		
War Diary	Sector		
Heading	War Diary 117 Coy. Machine Gun Corps 1 Nov-30 Nov 1917		
War Diary	Camp Near Brasserie At N 5d 99	01/11/1917	07/11/1917
War Diary	Tower Hamlets Sector	08/11/1917	11/11/1917
War Diary	Tower Hamlets Sector And Willebeek Camp N 9d 75	12/11/1917	12/11/1917
War Diary	Chippewa Camp	13/11/1917	15/11/1917
War Diary	Stirling Castle Coy H.Q. S 19b 35.85	15/11/1917	15/11/1917
War Diary	Polderhoek Sector	16/11/1917	19/11/1917
War Diary	Chippewa Camp (less Transport At Willebeek)	20/11/1917	24/11/1917
War Diary	Maxim Camp (L 13d 3.3)	25/11/1917	30/11/1917
Operation(al) Order(s)	Operation Order No. 11 By Capt L.E.H. Whitby.	14/11/1917	14/11/1917
Operation(al) Order(s)	Operation Order No. 9 By Capt L.E.H. Whitby.	03/11/1917	03/11/1917
Operation(al) Order(s)	Operation Order No. 10 By Capt L.E.H. Whitby.	15/11/1917	15/11/1917
Heading	1st Dec 1917 31st Dec War Diary 117 Coy. M.G.C.		
War Diary	Maxim Camp (L 13d 3.3)	01/12/1917	04/12/1917
War Diary	Watou Billets on Watou-Abeele Road (K 11.a And C)	05/12/1917	09/12/1917
War Diary	Waterdal	10/12/1917	29/12/1917
War Diary	Irish Fm (C 27a 15.50)	30/12/1917	30/12/1917
War Diary	Irish Fm	31/12/1917	31/12/1917
Operation(al) Order(s)	Operation Order No. 14	30/12/1917	30/12/1917
War Diary	Westroosebeke Sector	01/01/1918	08/01/1918
War Diary	Siege Camp (B 27a 76. Sheet 28)	09/01/1918	20/01/1918
War Diary	Road Camp (F 25c Sheet 27)	21/01/1918	21/01/1918
War Diary	Suzanne (Amiens 1/0,000)	25/01/1918	28/01/1918
War Diary	Moislans (Amiens 1/100,000)	29/01/1918	29/01/1918
War Diary	Fins (Valenciennes 1/100,000)	30/01/1918	31/01/1918
War Diary	Villers-Guislan Sector (Ref 57c SE 1/20,000)	31/01/1918	31/01/1918
War Diary	Villers Guislan Sector Ref Map 57c 1/20,000 And Villers Guislan 1/10,000	01/02/1918	23/02/1918
War Diary	Villers Guislain 1/10,000	24/02/1918	28/02/1918
Heading	WO95/2587/5		
Heading	117th Trench Mortar Bty Jly-Aug 1916		
Heading	117th Brigade Light Trench Mortar Battery July 1916		
War Diary	Festubert.	01/07/1916	13/07/1916
War Diary	Richebourg	14/07/1916	20/07/1916
War Diary	Le Touret	21/07/1916	24/07/1916
War Diary	Hamel	25/07/1916	26/07/1916
War Diary	Givenchy	27/07/1916	31/07/1916
Heading	117th Brigade Light Trench Mortar Battery August 1916		
War Diary	Givenchy	01/08/1916	31/08/1916

WO95/25874

39TH DIVISION

117TH INFY BDE

117TH MACHINE GUN COY.

MAY 1916-FEB 1918

117th Brigade.

39th Division.

Company disembarked HAVRE 16.5.16.

117th BRIGADE MACHINE GUN COMPANY

M A Y 1 9 1 6:

Army Form C. 2118.

Instructions regarding War Diaries and Intelligence Summaries are contained in F. S. Regs., Part II. and the Staff Manual respectively. Title Pages will be prepared in manuscript.

WAR DIARY
or
INTELLIGENCE SUMMARY
(Erase heading not required.)

Sheet No 1

Place	Date	Hour	Summary of Events and Information	Remarks and references to Appendices
HAVRE	16/5/16		Company entrained at GRANTHAM at 7 a.m on 15/5/16, embarked at SOUTHAMPTON same afternoon, disembarked at HAVRE on afternoon of 16th. In rest camp No 1.	A.N.H.
LE HAMEL (BETHUNE)	18/5/16		Entrained at HAVRE afternoon of 17th, arrived BETHUNE 3 p.m and proceeded to Billets at LE HAMEL.	A.N.H.
"	20/5/16		The 117th Brigade already had 6 officers and 104 other ranks calling themselves 117th Brigade Machine Gun Company. These were attached to 118th Machine Gun Company using their guns and acting as divisional troops.	
			Inspection at GORRE by G.O.C 117th Inf. Bde.	
			My officers were ordered to be attached to 118th M.G. Coy in the trench line for instruction & report.	
"	28/5/16		Under instructions from G.O.C 117th Brigade company reorganised as follows.	

2449 Wt. W14957/M90 750,000 1/16 J.B.C. & A. Forms/C.2118/12.

Army Form C. 2118.

WAR DIARY
or
INTELLIGENCE SUMMARY
(Erase heading not required.)

Instructions regarding War Diaries and Intelligence Summaries are contained in F. S. Regs., Part II. and the Staff Manual respectively. Title Pages will be prepared in manuscript.

Sheet 2

Place	Date	Hour	Summary of Events and Information	Remarks and references to Appendices
			Two sections formed out of the improvised company	
			The " " " " new company.	
			The surplus men of the improvised company returned to their battalions	
			" " " new company to remain attached till further orders.	
			The company moved to GORRE.	AAH
			G 31/5/15. A. Hall Hall Capt 117th Machine Gun Coy.	

117th Brigade.

39th Division.

117th BRIGADE MACHINE GUN COMPANY

J U N E 1 9 1 6

In the field
30/6/16.

D. A. G
3rd Ech.

Forwarded.

A Nall Nall Capt
Cdg 117 Bde M G Coy.

Instructions regarding War Diaries and Intelligence Summaries are contained in F. S. Regs., Part II. and the Staff Manual respectively. Title Pages will be prepared in manuscript.

WAR DIARY
or
INTELLIGENCE SUMMARY
(Erase heading not required.)

XXXIX Original

Army Form C. 2118.

117 M G Coy
Vol 2 Sheet 3
June

Place	Date	Hour	Summary of Events and Information	Remarks and references to Appendices
GIVENCHY	1/6/16		The Coy. took over the Machine Gun defence of GIVENCHY sector on 28/5/16 from 118th M.G. Coy. 8 guns were disposed in keeps in support line, ~~and~~ 4 in village line, and 4 in reserve at GORRE. Machine Gun headquarters in WESTMINSTER Br. Rd. in rear of village line. Section in reserve and village line relieved sections in support line every four days.	
"	5/6/16		A bombing raid was made by the brigade on night of the 4th-5th; 1 Gun under Lt. BARNETT and 1 gun 2Lt WILCOCK were brought up and fired over front line to assist in the barrage S. of the raided portion of the German trench, 1 gun under Lt WHYLEY assisted with indirect fire; 7000 rounds were fired from the three guns between 10.15pm and 10.45pm. Pte Done ~~attached~~ from 17th Sherwoods was wounded in left side.	39th Divl. Tactical Report attcd + numbered No 1
FERME du ROI	8/6/16		Relieved by 118th M.G. Coy + moved to billets at FERME du ROI near BETHUNE, for 8 days rest!	
LE HAMEL	10/6/16		Took over FESTUBERT sector from 106th M.G. Coy. 7 guns in support line 5 in village line, 4 in reserve with headquarters at LE HAMEL.	

2449 Wt. W14957/M90 750,000 1/16 J.B.C. & A. Forms/C.2118/12.

Instructions regarding War Diaries and Intelligence Summaries are contained in F. S. Regs., Part II. and the Staff Manual respectively. Title Pages will be prepared in manuscript.

WAR DIARY
or
INTELLIGENCE SUMMARY

(Erase heading not required.)

Army Form C. 2118.

Sheet 4

Place	Date	Hour	Summary of Events and Information	Remarks and references to Appendices
LOISNE	17/6/16		Headquarters and reserve section moved here on 1?/6/16. On 16/6/16 brigade took over additional 600 yds of line to the NORTH, 2 guns from the reserve section were utilized, leaving 2 guns only in reserve. Work being done by company usually consists of making range cards, plans + sketches, improving dugouts & emplacements. Two or three guns regularly fire about 1200 rounds ~~each~~ per gun per night indirect on German communication trenches and places where movement has been reported.	
LOISNE	30/6/16		On night of 29/30th June a smoke attack and bombing raid was made by the brigade. Two guns one under 2Lt Pearce, other under 2Lt Merchant were taken up to front line just N of the ISLANDS and assisted in barrage N. of the raiding party, firing through the smoke. 2Lt Bull was slightly wounded in upper lip by shell splinter. One gun under 2Lt Wilcock firing from DEAD COW assisted in barrage on S. of raiding party from 116th Brigade in RICHEBOURG.	

A. Hall Hall Capt
Cmdr 117th MGC

2449 Wt. W14957/M90 750,000 1/16 J.B.C. & A. Forms/C.2118/12.

117/Bde Machine Gun Co.

SECRET

War Diary

117th. Infantry Brigade.

Date 5 JUN 1916

No.

To/

Headquarters,

39th Division. No 1.

Tactical Progress Report 8 a.m. 4th June - 8 a.m. 5th June, 1916.

OPERATIONS

GIV. R

~~Full report~~. Full report of last Night's successful raid south of the DUCK'S BILL will follow. The party, consisting of 4 Officers and 70 men entered the enemy's trenches with comparative ease, except for a few bombs which the enemy ~~[illegible]~~ threw at our advancing party. Dug-outs were bombed, and a large number of the enemy accounted for.
The German artillery retaliation was slow for although the enemy sent up rockets almost as soon as our bombardment started it took twenty minutes before his artillery responded. KING'S Road, BERKELEY St, PICCADILLY, GIVENCHY KEEP and the Brickstacks were shelled during the retaliation with .77 mm, 4.2" and rum jars. About 50 M.G's were directed towards ORCHARD FARM - WINDY CORNER and WESTMINSTER BRIDGE Road.
Lewis Guns coooperated.
Our snipers claim two victims.

GIV L

~~[illegible]~~. Two mines were sprung by us near E sap (about A.9.d.16. 45). Correct coordinates to follow. The work of consolidating and connecting the craters was performed during the night and was quite successful.

Machine Gun. Co. M — No. 1 Gun in front line near ORCHARD Road fired 3,300 rounds between 10.17 and 10.50 p.m. traversing front and support line from Pt. 37 to Pt. 57.
No. 2 Gun in front line near FINCHLEY Road fired 2,050 rounds at same target and same time.
No. 3 Gun ORCHARD FARM fired 200 rounds between 10.17 and 10.47 at PLAIN ALLEY and TOWPATH ALLEY.

L.T.M. B. fired 260 rounds in accordance with the pre-arranged plan.

INTELLIGENCE

Two men seen at A.16.a.5.6. watching effects of anti-aircraft gun at ~~xx~~ 1.30 p.m. Dress - dark grey, with peaked caps.
Boards and wire supports being carried along PLAIN ALLEY.
Two men at A.10.a.7½.2. seen wearing civilian clothes.
Enemy's wire has been considerably strengthened from A.10.b.2.3. to A.10.d.6.9. At 3 a.m. enemy observed working opposite F Sap.

WORK

Repairs to parapet and damaged trenches. Shelters erected.

[signature]

Brig. Gen.
Commanding 117th. BRIGADE.

5th June, 1916.

H.H.

117th Brigade.

39th Division

9-------------

117th BRIGADE MACHINE GUN COMPANY

JULY 1916

Headquarters
117th Brigade

War Diary December

A. Alan Hall Capt

O.C. No. 117th Coy.
Machine Gun Corps.

Dec 3rd 1917

69

34 July

Army Form C. 2118.

117 M G Coy

Vol 3

WAR DIARY
or
INTELLIGENCE SUMMARY

(Erase heading not required.)

Instructions regarding War Diaries and Intelligence Summaries are contained in F. S. Regs., Part II. and the Staff Manual respectively. Title Pages will be prepared in manuscript.

Place	Date	Hour	Summary of Events and Information	Remarks and references to Appendices
LOISNE	11/7/16		One direct hit with H.E. on M.G. 15 emplacement which damaged the concrete roof. We fired 1200 rounds longe range fire from DEAD COW at BOARS HEAD between 10 + 11 p.m., 1000 rounds from TUBE KEEP on QUINQUE RUE between 12 midnight + 1 a.m., 450 rounds from TUBE KEEP on ADALBERT ALLEY between 1-35 and 2-5 a.m., 1450 rounds from OBL FIFE ROAD on ROCH ALLEY between 10-30 p.m. and 2-5 a.m.	
	12/7/16		Firing done 1000 rounds from FIFE ROAD on ENEMY SUPPORT LINES between 1-25 and 2 a.m. 1500 " " S. 27. a. 7½. 3½ on 28 A 5 2 5750 " " 21 A. 8.8 on ADALBERT ALLEY. The times of the two last mentioned firing are not given, as it was done as arranged with scheme.	
	13/7/16		Built up Emplacement at M.G 1 and M.G. 3, which were damaged by shell fire on the night of 12th/13th. Stripped roof of M.G. 15 under R.E's orders. Firing/	

2449 Wt. W14957/M90 750,000 1/16 J.B.C. & A. Forms/C.2118/12.

Army Form C. 2118.

Instructions regarding War Diaries and Intelligence Summaries are contained in F. S. Regs., Part II. and the Staff Manual respectively. Title Pages will be prepared in manuscript.

WAR DIARY
or
INTELLIGENCE SUMMARY

(Erase heading not required.)

Place	Date	Hour	Summary of Events and Information	Remarks and references to Appendices
LOISNE	13/7/16		Firing done	
			1700 rounds from DEAD COW to BOARS HEAD between 10 p.m. and 11.15 p.m.	
			1000 " " TUBE KEEP to ADALBERT ALLEY between 11-35 p.m. and 12-40 a.m.	
			1000 " " M.G.5 to GERMAN RESERVE TRENCHES in front of GIVENCHY between 1 and 2-10 a.m.	
	14/7/16		1000 " " M.G.R.3 to REDOUBT ALLEY N+S between 10-10 and 10-50 p.m.	
			1000 " " " " " " " BRICKFIELDS " 11-0 " 11-40 " "	
			750 " " " " " " " REDOUBT ALLEYS " 1-0 " 1-25 a.m.	
			750 " " " " " " " BRICKFIELDS " 1-35 " 1-55 " "	
			1000 " " DEAD COW " BOARS HEAD " 10-0 " 11-25 p.m.	
			1250 " " TUBE KEEP " ADALBERT ALLEY " 11-40 p.m. + 1 a.m.	
LE TOURET	16/7/16		On night of 15th/16th we were relieved at FESTUBERT by 118th M.G. Coy and took over RICHEBOURG sector from 184 M.G. Coy, 5 guns in front line, 5 guns in support line, 4 guns in WINDY CORNER line of Keeps, 2 guns in reserve at RICHEBOURG. Company H.Q. near LE TOURET Cemetery. Tactical work consisted of firing at gaps in wire with front line guns, and some overhead long range fire at night on communication.	

2449 Wt. W14957/M90 750,000 1/16 J.B.C. & A. Forms/C.2118/12.

Army Form C. 2118.

Instructions regarding War Diaries and Intelligence Summaries are contained in F. S. Regs., Part II. and the Staff Manual respectively. Title Pages will be prepared in manuscript.

WAR DIARY
or
INTELLIGENCE SUMMARY

(Erase heading not required.)

Place	Date	Hour	Summary of Events and Information	Remarks and references to Appendices
			communication trenches and roads.	
LE TOURET	17/7/16		Firing done	
			2000 rounds from S9a 1½ 7 to GERMAN COMM TRENCHES at intervals	
			3000 " " M.G. 3 " Gap in wire from S10d.77 to S11 a 22	
			2000 " " M. G. 7 " GAP in ENEMY WIRE from 10 p.m. to 4 a.m.	
			3500 " " M. G. 10 } FACTORY ST } " BOARS HEAD from 10 p.m. at intervals	
	18/7/16		1000 " " M. G. 7 " Gap in wire at S.16.A.7.2. Intervals during night	
			1000 " " M. G. 10 " " " " " S.16.A8.8 " " "	
			3000 " " M. G. 3 " Gaps " " from S. 11. a. 2½ to LATOURELLE CROSS ROADS Intervals during night	
	19/7/16		1250 " " M. G. 10 " Gap in wire S16 A 10.10 p.m. to 3-30 a.m.	
			1500 " " M. G. 7 " S16A gap in wire 10-30 " " 3-30 " "	
			2000 " " S.10.B.6 " continuation of RUE DE BOIS 10-30 p.m. to 2-30 a.m.	
			2000 " " M.G. 3 " Gap in wire S11 A2½ to LATOURELLE CROSS ROADS at intervals	
	20/7/16		1500 " " M. G. 7 " S16 d 7 2 gap at intervals	
			1450 " " M. G. 10 " S16 a 89 gap " "	
			2500 " " M. G. 3 " S11 a 22 to S10 d 67 gaps at intervals	
	21/7/16			

2449 Wt. W14957/M90 750,000 1/16 J.B.C. & A. Forms/C.2118/12.

Army Form C. 2118.

WAR DIARY
or
INTELLIGENCE SUMMARY
(Erase heading not required.)

Instructions regarding War Diaries and Intelligence Summaries are contained in F. S. Regs., Part II. and the Staff Manual respectively. Title Pages will be prepared in manuscript.

Place	Date	Hour	Summary of Events and Information	Remarks and references to Appendices
LACOUTURE	21/7/16		On 20/7/16 we were relieved at RICHEBOURG by 116th M.G. Coy. and proceeded to rest billets ¼ mile west of LACOUTURE.	
Le HAMEL	25/7/16.		On 24/7/16 moved to bivouack at LE HAMEL.	
GIVENCHY	27/7/16.		On 26/7/16 took over GIVENCHY section from 118th M.G. Coy. 6 guns in Keeps in support line, 4 guns in village line, 2 guns in reserve in village line, 4 guns in reserve at GORRE. Headquarters at PONT FIXE.	
			Firing done	
			500 rounds from O.F.3 to CANTELEUX ALLEY 10-5 to 10-15 p.m.	
			250 " " DFI. IFP " PLAIN ALLEY 10-30 p.m.	
			250 " " " " " TOWPATH ALLEY 10-40 p.m.	
			250 " " " " " CANTELEUR TRENCH 10-50 p.m.	
			250 " " O.F.3 " CUPOLA ALLEY 11-10 p.m.	
			250 " " " " CHAPELLE STROCH 11-20 p.m.	
			250 " " O.FI. IFP " TOWPATH ALLEY 11-40 p.m.	
			250 " " " " " PLAIN ALLEY 11-45 p.m.	
			250 " " " " " CHAPELLE STROCH 12-5 a.m.	
			500 " " O.F.3 " CANTELEUX at 12-20 a.m.	
			250/	

2449 Wt. W14957/M90 750,000 1/16 J.B.C. & A. Forms/C.2118/12.

Instructions regarding War Diaries and Intelligence Summaries are contained in F. S. Regs., Part II. and the Staff Manual respectively. Title Pages will be prepared in manuscript.

WAR DIARY
or
INTELLIGENCE SUMMARY
(Erase heading not required.)

Army Form C. 2118.

Place	Date	Hour	Summary of Events and Information	Remarks and references to Appendices
GIVENCHY	27/7/16		250 rounds from O.F.3 to CANTELEUX 1 a.m.	
			250 " " O.F.1. IFP to PLAIN ALLEY at 1-30 a.m.	
			250 " " O.F.3 " CANTELEUX ALLEY at 1-45 a.m.	
			250 " " " " CUPOLA ALLEY at 2.5 a.m.	
			2500 " " SPOILBANK to PLAIN ALLEY and TOWPATH ALLEY between 10.5 p.m. and 12.35 a.m.	
	28/7/16		250 " " O.F.3 to CUPOLA ALLEY at 10-45 p.m.	
			250 " " " " " " " 11-0 p.m.	
			250 " " " " CHAPELLE STROCH at 11-10 p.m.	
			250 " " SPOILBANK to TOWPATH ALLEY at 11-45 p.m.	
			250 " " " " PLAIN ALLEY " 12-0 p.m.	
			250 " " O.F.3. to CANTELEUX ALLEYS " 12-45 a.m.	
			250 " " " " CUPOLA ALLEY " 12-50 a.m.	
			250 " " " " CANTELEUX at 1 a.m.	
			250 " " SPOILBANK to TOWPATH ALLEY at 1-20 a.m.	
			250 " " " " PLAIN ALLEY at 1-30 a.m.	
	29/7/16		250 " " " KEEP to PLAIN ALLEY at 1-20 a.m.	
			250 " " " " " TOWPATH ALLEY at 1-30 a.m.	
	30/7/16			

2449 Wt. W14957/M90 750,000 1/16 J.B.C. & A. Forms/C.2118/12.

Army Form C. 2118.

WAR DIARY
or
INTELLIGENCE SUMMARY
(Erase heading not required.)

Instructions regarding War Diaries and Intelligence Summaries are contained in F. S. Regs., Part II. and the Staff Manual respectively. Title Pages will be prepared in manuscript.

Place	Date	Hour	Summary of Events and Information	Remarks and references to Appendices
GIVENCHY	30/7/16		Firing done	
			250 rounds from O.F.3 to CUPOLA ALLEY at 10-45 p.m.	
			250 " " " " " " 11-0 p.m.	
			250 " " " " CHAPELLE STROCH at 11-10 p.m.	
			250 " " SPOILBANK to TOWPATH ALLEY at 11-45 p.m.	
			250 " " " " PLAIN ALLEY at 12 p.m.	
			250 " " O.F.3 to CANTELEUX ALLEY at 12-45 a.m.	
			250 " " " " CUPOLA ALLEY at 12-50 a.m.	
			250 " " " " CANTELEUX ALLEY at 1 a.m.	
			250 " " SPOILBANK to TOWPATH ALLEY at 1-20 a.m.	
			250 " " " " PLAIN ALLEY at 1-30 a.m.	
	31/7/16		750 " " A.15.a55 to A10a72 to A4d36.	
			500 " " SPOILBANK to TOWPATH ALLEY	
			250 " " " " PLAIN ALLEY	
			250 " " O.F.3 to CUPOLA ALLEY	
			500 " " " " CHAPELLE STROCH	
			250 " " " " CANTELEUX	
			250 " " " " CHAPELLE STROCH	
			250 " " SPOILBANK to PLAIN ALLEY	

A. Hall Hall Capt.
O.C. No. [illegible] Coy.
Machine Gun Corps.

2449 Wt. W14957/M90 750,000 1/16 J.B.C. & A. Forms/C.2118/12.

117th Brigade.

39th Division.

117th BRIGADEMACHINE GUN COMPANY

AUGUST 1 9 1 6

Instructions regarding War Diaries and Intelligence Summaries are contained in F. S. Regs., Part II. and the Staff Manual respectively. Title Pages will be prepared in manuscript.

WAR DIARY
or
INTELLIGENCE SUMMARY

(Erase heading not required.)

Lt Kolb Aug '16 116 MGC Vol 4

Army Form C. 2118.

Place	Date	Hour	Summary of Events and Information	Remarks and references to Appendices
GIVENCHY	1/8		Company cooperated in the raid by 16th Notts + Derby Regt by long range searching fire on enemy trenches. One gun of 116th M.G.C. cooperated by firing on CANTELEUX ALLEY NORTH	
			Time / From / At / Rounds	
			11.40 pm to 1.55 am / ORCHARD FARM / CANTELEUX ALLEYS N + S / 7250	
			" " / WINDY CORNER / CHAPELLE St ROCHE / 3500	
"	2/8, 3/8, 4/8, 5/8		Engaged targets as under with indirect fire between 9.30 pm and 1 am 5000 rounds CANTELEUX ALLEYS N+S CHAPELLE St ROCHE, PLAIN ALLEY, TOWPATH ALLEY	
BETHUNE	6/8		Relieved by 116th MG Coy. and went to rest billets at ECOLE de JEUNE FILLES, BETHUNE	
	7/8		About 10 heavy shells dropped in BETHUNE + the Coy moved out of the town during the shelling.	
	8/8, 9/8		Training	
AUCHEL	10/8		Company marched to AUCHEL	
ROCOURT	11/8		" " " ROCOURT	
ORLENCOURT	12/8		" " " ORLENCOURT	

2449 Wt. W14957/M90 750,000 1/16 J.B.C. & A. Forms/C.2118/12.

Army Form C. 2118.

Instructions regarding War Diaries and Intelligence Summaries are contained in F. S. Regs., Part II. and the Staff Manual respectively. Title Pages will be prepared in manuscript.

WAR DIARY
or
INTELLIGENCE SUMMARY
(Erase heading not required.)

Place	Date	Hour	Summary of Events and Information	Remarks and references to Appendices
	1916			
ORLENCOURT	13/8		Training	
"	14/8		Training on the MONCHY BRETON training area	
"	15/8		" " " " " " 2Lts Stewart + Hasler joined the Coy.	
	16/8		" " " " " "	
	17/8		" " " " " "	
	19/8		" " " " " "	
	20/8		" " " " " " Commenced rehearsals of assault on BOSCHE trenches	
	21/8		" " " " " " continued " " "	
			Lieuts Marsden (2nd in Command) + Dunn (attd.) ordered to Grantham. ~~[illegible]~~	
	22/8		Training + rehearsals of assault continued	
MAISNIL-ST-POL	23/8		company marched to MAISNIL ST POL	
LA CLOSERIE Fm	24/8		" " " LA CLOSERIE FERME	
VAUCHELLES	25/8		" " " VACHELLES-LES-AUTHIE.	
"	26/8		Rest.	
	27/8		O.C. Coy + O.C. No 3 section went to reconnoitre trench line.	
BERTRANCOURT	28/8		company marched to BERTRANCOURT	
"	29/8		Training and rest	
"	30/8		" " "	
"	31/8		" " "	

A. Hall Hall Capt
Cmdg 117 MG Coy.

2449 Wt. W14957/M90 750,000 1/16 J.B.C. & A. Forms/C.2118/12.

117th Brigade.

39th Division.

117th BRIGADE MACHINE GUN COMPANY

SEPTEMBER 1 9 1 6 :

Army Form C. 2118.

Vol 5

Instructions regarding War Diaries and Intelligence Summaries are contained in F. S. Regs., Part II. and the Staff Manual respectively. Title Pages will be prepared in manuscript.

WAR DIARY
or
INTELLIGENCE SUMMARY

(Erase heading not required.)

117 MGC

Place	Date	Hour	Summary of Events and Information	Remarks and references to Appendices
BERTRANCOURT	1/9/16		Training and rest	
"	~~2/9/16~~ 4/9/16		Company moved in afternoon of 2nd, No 1 Section with 16th Rifle Brigade, No 3 Section with 17th Notts and Derby and remained with them throughout the operations. Nos 2 + 4 sections moved at 3 p.m. to VITERMONT rested 2 hours there and had tea, then proceeded to KNIGHTSBRIDGE via MESNIL arriving 9 p.m. Proceeded by overland route 11th to GABION AVENUE, No 4 Section to FORT JACKSON to be in reserve, and No 2 section with O.C. Coy. CSM + signallers to dugouts in SHOOTERS HILL and FRENCH TRENCH.	
			The 16th Rifle Brigade on the right and 17th Notts + Derby on the left were to assault the enemys trenches and were each allotted one section of M.G. Coy to go over + consolidate. Brigade Operation Order + Coy Operation Order attached, also report of operations.	
			~~The brigade was relieved on~~ Casualties most of which occurred during the shelling of the trenches after return of the assaulting party were Lt Pearce killed ~~Lieut~~ Lt Brown wounded in leg, Lt Stewart wounded in shoulder, Sergt Baxter killed, 24 ~~[illegible]~~ O.Ran. wounded and 5 missing.	
			The brigade was relieved in the evening of 3/9/16 and we returned to our camp at BERTRANCOURT	
	5/9/16			

2449 Wt. W14957/M90 750,000 1/16 J.B.C. & A. Forms/C.2118/12.

Army Form C. 2118.

WAR DIARY
or
INTELLIGENCE SUMMARY
(Erase heading not required.)

Instructions regarding War Diaries and Intelligence Summaries are contained in F. S. Regs., Part II. and the Staff Manual respectively. Title Pages will be prepared in manuscript.

Place	Date	Hour	Summary of Events and Information	Remarks and references to Appendices
BERTRANCOURT	5/9/16		Rest	
MAILLY - MAILLET	6/9/16		Moved from BERTRANCOURT to take over part of the line from 144th Brigade. No 4 section in support line. 2 guns of No 1 Section at FORT ANLIN, Remainder of company in reserve at MAILLY, Transport at BEAUSSART.	
"	7/9/16		The neighbourhood of MAILLY-MAILLET was shelled at intervals during the day & night. Work done Emplacements improved & repaired. New alternative emplacement (open) built at FORT ANLEY. Plans, sectors, etc Commenced for all emplacements. Ammunition cleaned & boxes sealed. Tactics 1500 Rounds fired on Enemy wire in Square 17 A, between 9.30pm till 4.30 am	
"	8/9/16		BERTRANCOURT shelled at about 1.0 pm. Enemy sent over miniature balloons during the afternoon & evening, which dropped at intervals copies of a French paper viz JOURNAL D'ARDENNES. Work done Improving & repairing of M.G. emplacements carried on, etc. Tactics 1000 Rounds fired at intervals during the night at BEAUMONT HAMEL. Also 1000 Rounds fired at Gaps in enemy wire	

2449 Wt. W14957/M90 750,000 1/16 J.B.C. & A. Forms/C.2118/12.

Instructions regarding War Diaries and Intelligence Summaries are contained in F. S. Regs., Part II. and the Staff Manual respectively. Title Pages will be prepared in manuscript.

WAR DIARY
or
INTELLIGENCE SUMMARY

(Erase heading not required.)

Place	Date	Hour	Summary of Events and Information	Remarks and references to Appendices
MAILLY-MALLET	9/6/16		The neighbourhood of MAILLY MAILLET was lightly shelled at intervals during day. Work done. Work on improving emplacements continued. 1 Gun mounted at FORT ANLEY against enemy aircraft. Tasks. 1000 Rounds fired on WAGGON ROAD. 1400 Rounds on gaps in enemy wire. 1000 Rounds on BEAUMONT HAMEL.	
"	10/6/16		The neighbourhood of MAILLY MAILLET shelled at [illegible] during day & night. Work done. [illegible] emplacements continued. Tasks. 1500 Rounds [illegible] GAPS IN ENEMY WIRE [illegible]. 1500 Rounds [illegible] on WAGGON ROAD.	
"	11/6/16		MAILLY MAILLET shelled [illegible] during the night. [illegible] about 5 a.m. for 15 minutes. Enemy [illegible] number of [illegible]. Work done. [illegible] Aircraft Gun at FORT ANLEY. Tasks. 1000 Rounds on GAPS IN ENEMY WIRE. 1000 Rounds on Waggon Road.	

2449 Wt. W14957/M90 750,000 1/16 J.B.C. & A. Forms/C.2118/12.

WAR DIARY
or
INTELLIGENCE SUMMARY
(Erase heading not required.)

Instructions regarding War Diaries and Intelligence Summaries are contained in F. S. Regs., Part II. and the Staff Manual respectively. Title Pages will be prepared in manuscript.

Place	Date	Hour	Summary of Events and Information	Remarks and references to Appendices
MAILLY-MAILLET	12/9/16		MAILLY MAILLET shelled at intervals during day. Road from MESNIL to KNIGHTSBRIDGE shelled heavily from 9.0 - 9.30 a.m. Enemy Artillery active all day. Work done. Improvement of emplacements continued. Dugouts cleaned, ammunition cleaned etc. Tactics. 1000 Rounds fired on WAGGON ROAD. 1000 Rounds fired on GAPS IN ENEMY WIRE. 1000 Rounds fired on BEAUMONT ALLEY.	
"	13/9/16		Enemy quiet during day. Enemy machine guns fairly active during night. Work done. Work on improvement & rebuilding of emplacements continued. Tactics. 1000 Rounds fired on WAGGON ROAD. 1000 Rounds on BEAUMONT ALLEY. 1000 Rounds on Gaps in wire at Q17.d 8[?].8[?]	
"	14/9/16		A heavy Bombardment took place on our right about 8.0 pm & enemy sent up a number of Red & Green lights in bouquets of varying numbers. Enemy M. G's very active all day against our aeroplanes. Work done. Section relief took place. Places for three (3) emplacements made. New emplacement made for [illegible]. Dug out for night firing team commenced.	

2449 Wt. W14957/M90 750,000 1/16 J.B.C. & A. Forms/C.2118/12.

Instructions regarding War Diaries and Intelligence Summaries are contained in F. S. Regs., Part II. and the Staff Manual respectively. Title Pages will be prepared in manuscript.

WAR DIARY
or
INTELLIGENCE SUMMARY

(Erase heading not required.)

Place	Date	Hour	Summary of Events and Information	Remarks and references to Appendices
MAILLY/MALLET	14/9/16		Tactics. 750 Rounds fired at Gaps in wire. 1500 Rounds indirect fired at WAGGON ROAD. Right Front four Guns fired 2000 Rounds at GERMAN SUPPORT + RESERVE LINES. N of Y RAVINE. Left forward Guns fired 4200 Rounds at TRENCHES N of Q17 6o4-14-94. FORT ANLEY Gun fired 3000 Rounds on LOWER portion of WAGGON ROAD + adjoining TRENCHES + Y RAVINE. 2 Guns at Night firing position in St JOHN'S ROAD fired 3500 at upper portion of WAGGON ROAD + BEAUMONT ALLEY. Heavy shelling experienced at HAYMARKET + fairly heavy at St JOHNS ROAD + FETHARD St.	
"	15/9/16		Enemy M.G. active during night. Enemy [illegible] shelled at midnight. Enemy artillery did not reply. Work done. Emplacements cleaned + repaired. Ammunition cleaned + Belts refilled. Building of new emplacements (continued). Tactics. 1250 Rounds fired at gaps in heavy wire in Q17 2000. Rounds fired at WAGGON ROAD + adjoining COMMUNICATION TRENCHES.	
	16/9/16		MAILLY MALLET fairly heavily shelled 9.30 + 10.30 pm. 2/Lt PRATT R.E. (Transport Officer) wounded outside the Coy H.Q. His Pony killed.	

2449 Wt. W14957/M90 750,000 1/16 J.B.C. & A. Forms/C.2118/12.

WAR DIARY
or
INTELLIGENCE SUMMARY

(Erase heading not required.)

Instructions regarding War Diaries and Intelligence Summaries are contained in F. S. Regs., Part II. and the Staff Manual respectively. Title Pages will be prepared in manuscript.

Place	Date	Hour	Summary of Events and Information	Remarks and references to Appendices
MAILLY MAILLET	16/9/16		A billet in MAILLY MAILLET was set on fire by enemy shells at 9.30 p.m. WORK DONE. Emplacements & dugouts cleaned & repaired. S.A.A. cleaned & belts refilled. TACTICS 500 Rounds fired on WAGGON ROAD. 1500 Rounds fired on gaps in ENEMY WIRE in Q17 a & c [illegible]	
"	17/9/16 (17 written over 18)		MAILLY MAILLET shelled during morning & night. Quiet on our front all day. WORK DONE. Dugouts & emplacements cleaned & repaired. TACTICS 1500 Rounds at WAGGON ROAD & adjoining communication trenches.	
"	18/9/16	-	Fairly quiet all day. Enemy machine guns active during night. Work done Improvements on emplacements in PARK LANE & ST. JOHN'S ROAD, & of Officers dugout in UXBRIDGE, continued.	

Instructions regarding War Diaries and Intelligence Summaries are contained in F. S. Regs., Part II. and the Staff Manual respectively. Title Pages will be prepared in manuscript.

WAR DIARY or INTELLIGENCE SUMMARY

(Erase heading not required.)

Place	Date	Hour	Summary of Events and Information	Remarks and references to Appendices
MAILLY MALLET	18.9.16		Tactics 750 Rounds fired at WAGGON ROAD. 750 " " " Gaps in Enemy wire	
	19.9.16		The Company moved from MAILLY-MALLET to BERTRANCOURT. Nos 1 & 3 Sections remained behind in the line, under the Command of 118 Coy.	
	20/9/16		Took over HEBUTERNE section from 99th Brigade, & SERRE section from 6th Bde, Each of these Brigades leaving 2 sections of their M G Coy in the line, & 117 Coy putting 1 section in each Brigade Front. 3 Guns of No 3 Battery MMG. also occupied position in HEBUTERNE Section. Coy H.Q at COURCELLE. Transport &c at BEAUSSART.	
COURCELLE-AU-BOIS.	20.9.16		BERTRANCOURT. was shelled about 3.30 pm. Fairly quiet on our front. Work done. Emplacements etc taken over from 99th & 6th M.G. Co's Dugouts & emplacements cleaned, making of Range cards, Plans, Sectors, etc ,, Commenced. Tactics. 500 Rounds fired on Gaps in Enemy wire at K17d28	
"	21.9.16		Fairly quiet all day. A big explosion, apparently a mine, took place, some distance down south. Enemy machine Guns fairly active all night. Work done. Ammunition cleaned. Work on Range Cards etc Continued.	

2449 Wt. W14957/M90 750,000 1/16 J.B.C. & A. Forms/C.2118/12.

Instructions regarding War Diaries and Intelligence Summaries are contained in F. S. Regs., Part II. and the Staff Manual respectively. Title Pages will be prepared in manuscript.

or

INTELLIGENCE SUMMARY

(Erase heading not required.)

Place	Date	Hour	Summary of Events and Information	Remarks and references to Appendices
COURCELLE	21/9/16		TACTICS. 500 Rounds fired on GAPS in wire at K17. d 28 — .	
-do-	22/9/16		Our aircraft dropped bombs on Enemy Front Line. E of HEBUTERNE. 3 Enemy were reported to have been carried in from his wire early this morning. 8.0 am to 10.30 am, a hostile Aeroplane reconnoitred from HEBUTRNE Southwards. Type of machine not known (Biplane)	
			Tactics 1000 Rounds fired at GAP in wire @ K17 b 04. 1000 " " " " " " K23 d 86. 2800 " " " SERRE. 100 " " " Enemy aircraft.	
			Work done. Emplacements & dugouts cleaned & repaired New emplacements under RE Supervision Continued	
do	23/9/16		The neighbourhood of COURCELLE was shelled during the day. Enemy M Gs fairly active during the ~~day~~ night. Hostile Aircraft seen at 9 30 am & 5.30pm. Two of the guns left under the Command of 118 Coy were damaged by a shell bursting	

Instructions regarding War Diaries and Intelligence Summaries are contained in F. S. Regs., Part II. and the Staff Manual respectively. Title Pages will be prepared in manuscript.

or

INTELLIGENCE SUMMARY

(Erase heading not required.)

Place	Date	Hour	Summary of Events and Information	Remarks and references to Appendices
	23/9		in the recess where they were kept during the day. 6 men suffered from shell shock & bruises from this cause. 1500 Rounds fired at Gap K23d8. 500 " " " Enemy aircraft.	
COURCELLE	24/9		Enemy aeroplane seen over our lines at 6.30pm. Quiet during day. About 9.30pm gun position in WRANGLE AVENUE was shelled. Enemy M Gs active during night. 3000 Rds fired at Gap in wire K23d8. 1700 " " " " " " K17b6. 1500 " " " " " " K17b23. 500 " " " Enemy aircraft.	
"	25/9/16		Enemy aircraft busy during day. 4 were seen over COURCELLE about 12.0 midday, proceeding in a S.E. direction. Artillery Bombardments at 8.30 & 10.0pm. The Coy co-operated in a raid carried out by 1st KRRCs at 10.0pm, by indirect & direct fire on Gaps in wire & Communication trenches.	

2449 Wt. W14957/M90 750,000 1/16 J.B.C. & A. Forms/C.2118/12.

WAR DIARY
or
INTELLIGENCE SUMMARY
(Erase heading not required.)

Instructions regarding War Diaries and Intelligence Summaries are contained in F. S. Regs., Part II. and the Staff Manual respectively. Title Pages will be prepared in manuscript.

Place	Date	Hour	Summary of Events and Information	Remarks and references to Appendices
COURCELLE	26/9/16		7000 Rounds fired at Gaps from K17d28 to K17b02	
			5750 " " " " " K17b05 to K17b02	
			1950 " " " " " K23d7 to K23b5.6.	
			4000 " " " " " K23b64 to THE POINT.	
			4000 " " " " " K17d28. to THE POINT	
			5000 " " " " " K23d8½ 4½.	
			1400 " " " Enemy aircraft.	
"	27/9/16		Our lines were lightly shelled about 2-30 and 5-0 p.m. Enemy Field Guns and machine Guns fairly active all night.	
			6000 Rounds fired at SERRE	
			6500 " " " Comm. Trenches from K24a63 and K24c85.	
			12,500 " " " LA LOUVIERE FARM	
			13,000 " " " SUNKEN ROAD	
			5,000 " " " Gaps in wire	
			500 " " " Enemy aircraft.	
"	28/9/16		Heavy bombardment on right and left during night. 2 German planes seen in a N.E. direction at 5 p.m. very high up. Shells fell near R. sector H.Q. at 12 a.m. New N.F. emplacement at STAFF COPSE shelled during the day. Enemy M. Gs very active all	

2449 Wt. W14957/M90 750,000 1/16 J.B.C. & A. Forms/C.2118/12.

Instructions regarding War Diaries and Intelligence Summaries are contained in F. S. Regs., Part II. and the Staff Manual respectively. Title Pages will be prepared in manuscript.

WAR DIARY
or
INTELLIGENCE SUMMARY
(Erase heading not required.)

Place	Date	Hour	Summary of Events and Information	Remarks and references to Appendices
			all day against our aircraft.	
			8,000 Rounds fired at SERRE	
			2,500 " " " GAP K17a. 28.	
			2,500 " " " K.17b.a.2	
			2,500 " " " Comm. Trenches from K24 a 6.3.	
			3,000 " " " LA LOUVIERE FARM.	
			5,000 " " " GAPS K23d–	
COURCELLE	29/9/16		Enemy M.G's were active all day against our aircraft. Our artillery opened a heavy bombardment on the right at 1-0 p.m., also at 11-25 p.m. Our airmen brought down a German plane which fell in SERRE.	
			2,000 Rounds fired at Gap at K17d. 28 to Point 02	
			2,000 " " " " K17b.05 " Point 02	
			500 " " " Enemy aircraft	
			3,000 " " " Gap K23 d 8.4.	
"	30/9/16		Our artillery opened a heavy fire about midday. Otherwise quiet. Very misty. Gun emplacement at WRANGLE AVENUE was shelled.	

2449 Wt. W14957/M90 750,000 1/16 J.B.C. & A. Forms/C.2118/12.

Instructions regarding War Diaries and Intelligence Summaries are contained in F. S. Regs., Part II. and the Staff Manual respectively. Title Pages will be prepared in manuscript.

or

INTELLIGENCE SUMMARY

(Erase heading not required.)

Place	Date	Hour	Summary of Events and Information	Remarks and references to Appendices
			shelled with HE Shrapnel 7-8 p.m. Enemy M.G. fairly active during the night.	
			1,000 Rounds fired at GAP K23 d 8.4.	
			" " " " K17 d 28.	
			2,500 " " " K17 b 12.	
			2,000 " " " K24 a 63.	
			2,500 " " "	
			No 4 section was relieved by 99th M.G. Coy in SERRE sector.	
			A. Hall Hall Capt	

2449 Wt. W14957/M90 750,000 1/16 J.B.C. & A. Forms/C.2118/12.

117th Brigade

39th Division.

117th BRIGADE MACHINE GUN COMPANY

OCTOBERB 1 9 1 6

Army Form C. 2118.
VOL 6

Instructions regarding War Diaries and Intelligence Summaries are contained in F. S. Regs., Part II. and the Staff Manual respectively. Title Pages will be prepared in manuscript.

WAR DIARY
or
~~INTELLIGENCE~~ SUMMARY
(Erase heading not required.)

117th Company Machine Gun Corps

Place	Date	Hour	Summary of Events and Information	Remarks and references to Appendices
COURCELLE	1/10/16		No 2 Section in HEBUTERNE Sector was relieved by 6 M. G. Co. Company moved into Z Camp BERTRANCOURT.	
BERTRANCOURT MARTINSART	2/10/16		The Company moved into MARTINSART. MARTINSART was shelled during the night. No 1 + 3 Sections were relieved in the HAMEL sector by 116 + 118 M G Cos.	
MARTINSART.	3/10/16		The Company moved into hutments + Bivouacs in MARTINSART WOODS.	
"	4/10/16		The company relieved 54th 55 M.G. Coy ~~went into trenches~~ in THIEPVAL Sector. Coy H.Q. in dugouts at AUTHUILLE WOOD. All 16 Guns in the line. Coy advanced H.Q. in dugout in THIEPVAL.	
THIEPVAL	5/10/16		Enemy shelled our lines all night + day. AUTHUILLE WOOD was shelled during the night.	
"	6/10/16		Enemy shelled our lines continuously. Gun + tripod at Point 64 blown up by a 77 mm. shell + one man killed. AUTHUILLE WOOD shelled during the day. 1000 Rounds fired on Enemy trenches NORTH of R. ANCRE. ~~[illegible]~~	
"	7/10/16		Throughout the day the enemy's Artillery was fairly active. From 7.0 - 9.0 pm the Enemy Artillery greatly increased in activity ~~on~~ + our front and Communication trenches were heavily shelled by 77mm + 5.9". Again between 4.0 + 6.0 am their artillery was very active, gradually	

2449 Wt. W14957/M90 750,000 1/16 J.B.C. & A. Forms/C.2118/12.

Army Form C. 2118.

Instructions regarding War Diaries and Intelligence Summaries are contained in F. S. Regs., Part II. and the Staff Manual respectively. Title Pages will be prepared in manuscript.

WAR DIARY
or
~~INTELLIGENCE SUMMARY~~
(Erase heading not required.)

Place	Date	Hour	Summary of Events and Information	Remarks and references to Appendices
THIEPVAL	7/10/16		decreasing in intensity. Two tripods, at gun positions in our Front line immediately S. of the R. ANCRE. were buried by shell fire, one of which has not yet been recovered. The enemy attacked SCHWABEN REDOUBT during the night, but were repulsed and about 12 prisoners taken. WORK DONE. Dugouts cleaned, + emplacements repaired as far as possible. New latrine built at No 2 Gun position. TACTICS. 2500 Rounds fired at Enemy Front + Communication Trenches N. of R. ANCRE.	
"	~~7/10/16~~		Two guns of No 3 Section under L/Sergt Hollywell and L/Corpl Shaw got into action and fired 4 belts at close range causing considerable casualties to the enemy.	
"	8/10/16		Infantry attacked northern part of the SCHWABEN REDOUBT, but failed to hold it. Guns acted in accordance with attached copy of operation order ... Enemy artillery active all day against our front + Communication trenches. AUTHUILLE WOOD was shelled during the night. Enemy M.G.s active at intervals during night. Coy co-operated with 7th Division in the capture of STUFF REDOUBT, by indirect fire on Communication trenches. 1000 Rounds fired on STRASBURG TRENCH 2500 " " " LUCKY WAY 1000 " " " VALLEY in R.1. 1500 " " " TRENCHES N of R. ANCRE	

2449 Wt. W14957/M90 750,000 1/16 J.B.C. & A. Forms/C.2118/12.

Army Form C. 2118.

WAR DIARY
or
INTELLIGENCE SUMMARY
(Erase heading not required.)

Instructions regarding War Diaries and Intelligence Summaries are contained in F. S. Regs., Part II. and the Staff Manual respectively. Title Pages will be prepared in manuscript.

Place	Date	Hour	Summary of Events and Information	Remarks and references to Appendices
THIEPVAL	9/10/16	–	Enemy artillery very active all over Front line, THIEPVAL & THIEPVAL WOOD. Some lachrymatory shells fell at THIEPVAL during the night. 1500 Rounds fired on LUCKY WAY 1500 " " " TRENCHES N of the R ANCRE 500 " " " STRASBOURG TRENCH.	
"	10/10/16		The Company was relieved by the 118 Coy, & proceeded to billets in MARTINSART WOODS.	
MARTINSART	14/10/16		6 Guns sent up to HAMEL to provide Barrage fire on trenches S of R. ANCRE.	
"	16/10/16		Company moved in trenches S of ANCRE. Coy HQ established at NORTH BLUFFS. AUTVILLE.	
AUTHUILLE	17.10.16		N of ANCRE, enemy artillery active throughout the day & night. S of ANCRE Enemy M.G. fairly active during the night. The neighbourhood of N. BLUFFS & AUTHUILLE was shelled during the night. THIEPVAL WOOD was	

2449 Wt. W14957/M90 750,000 1/16 J.B.C. & A. Forms/C.2118/12.

Instructions regarding War Diaries and Intelligence Summaries are contained in F. S. Regs., Part II. and the Staff Manual respectively. Title Pages will be prepared in manuscript.

Army Form C. 2118.

WAR DIARY
or
~~INTELLIGENCE SUMMARY~~
(Erase heading not required.)

Place	Date	Hour	Summary of Events and Information	Remarks and references to Appendices
			shelled fairly heavily during the night & there was intermittent shelling throughout the night on the remainder of the sector. Very light fired from enemy front line opposite THIEPVAL WOOD fell right in our trenches near POINT 86. 1000. Rounds fired at Enemy trenches N of R. ANCRE.	
AUTHUILLE	18/10/16		N of ANCRE Intermittent shelling throughout the day & night. S of ANCRE Very heavy shelling during the afternoon on our Front & Support Lines. Intermittent shelling during the night. N. BLUFFS were shelled at intervals during the night. 2000 Rounds fired at Communication Trenches N of ANCRE.	
"	19/10/16		N of ANCRE. Enemy artillery active throughout the night S of ANCRE The neighbourhood of N BLUFFS was shelled at intervals during the night. Enemy artillery active all night. Neighbourhood of POINTS, 86 & 91 shelled heavily during the afternoon Enemy M.G.s fairly active at night. Guns N of ANCRE fired 2500 Rounds at BEAUCOURT. 2000 " " Communication trenches from R13 c4.8 to R13 b2.4. " S of ANCRE " 1000 " " trenches N of ANCRE.	
"	20/10/16		N of ANCRE. – Gas shells fell near PROSPECT TRENCH at 12.15 to 12.30 am A bright light was seen in enemy trenches at 7.30 pm at R9 c60	

Instructions regarding War Diaries and Intelligence Summaries are contained in F. S. Regs., Part II. and the Staff Manual respectively. Title Pages will be prepared in manuscript.

WAR DIARY
or
~~INTELLIGENCE~~ SUMMARY
(Erase heading not required.)

Army Form C. 2118.

Place	Date	Hour	Summary of Events and Information	Remarks and references to Appendices
	20/10/16		S of ANCRE. Heavy Bombardment on our front lines about 8.0 am. Enemy artillery active all night. Enemy MG's active at intervals during the night. 1000 Rounds fired at Q17.b 2.2 2500 " " " BEAUCOURT 2000 " " " VALLEY in R14.	
AUTHUILLE	21/10/16		N of ANCRE At 7.35pm last night & at 5.10 am this morning the S.O.S was observed, & these six guns opened fire on their barrage lines. S of ANCRE. Intermittent shelling throughout the day. Heavy shelling on our front line about 8.0 last night & from 5.0 - 6.0 this morning, including a few Gas Shells. Gas Helmets were worn in the front line for 1 hour. Guns S of Ancre. fired 1000 rounds at Q 17 b 2.2 " N of Ancre. " 15000 " on Barrage lines " " " 8000 " " new trench from R19 a 8.9. " " " 2500 " " HANSA LINE.	
"	22/10/16		N of R ANCRE Intermittent shelling throughout the night	

2449 Wt. W14957/M90 750,000 1/16 J.B.C. & A. Forms/C.2118/12.

WAR DIARY
or
~~INTELLIGENCE SUMMARY~~
(Erase heading not required.)

Army Form C. 2118.

Instructions regarding War Diaries and Intelligence Summaries are contained in F. S. Regs., Part II. and the Staff Manual respectively. Title Pages will be prepared in manuscript.

Place	Date	Hour	Summary of Events and Information	Remarks and references to Appendices
AUTHUILLE	22/10/16		S of R ANCRE. NORTH BLUFFS & neighborhood were shelled during the night. Heavy shelling on our front & support lines during the day. Gas Shells fell in THIEPVAL WOOD yesterday. Fairly quiet during the night, beyond a desultory bombardment between 8.0 & 9.0 pm.	
			Guns N of ANCRE. fired 8000 Rounds on Barrage Lines	
			5000 " Trench from R 19 a 5.8	
			5000 " ST PIERRE DIVION.	
			5000 " BEAUCOURT SUR ANCRE.	
			5000 " SERB ROAD.	
			Guns S of ANCRE 1000 " Q 19 C 3.5	
			4000 " Q 18 [illegible]	
AUTHUILLE	23/10/16		Six Guns N of R ANCRE relieved by 34 M G Co. No 4 Section relieved one Section of 116 Coy in SCHWABEN REDOUBT. Intermittent Artillery activity all day. Fairly heavy Bombardment about 5.30 pm on our front & support lines, also at 6.30 am. this morning, lasting for about 1 hour in each case.	

2449 Wt. W14957/M90 750,000 1/16 J.B.C. & A. Forms/C.2118/12.

Instructions regarding War Diaries and Intelligence Summaries are contained in F. S. Regs., Part II. and the Staff Manual respectively. Title Pages will be prepared in manuscript.

WAR DIARY
or
~~INTELLIGENCE~~ SUMMARY
(Erase heading not required.)

Army Form C. 2118.

Place	Date	Hour	Summary of Events and Information	Remarks and references to Appendices
AUTHUILLE	23/10/16		2000 Rounds fired at Q 24 d 2.2 to Q 17 b 2.2.	
"	24/10/16		Usual Artillery Activity during the day. Heavy bombardments on Front & Support lines, between 2.30 – 4.0 pm & 6.0 to 8.0 pm. Fairly quiet during the night. Lachrymatory shells were dropped in THIEPVAL WOOD at dusk and at dawn. Gas helmets were worn for 1 hour on both occasions. 1500 Rounds were fired at HANSA ROAD. 5000 " " " " Q 24 b 9.3	
"	25/10/16		Enemy Artillery active all day & night. A few gas shells were put into THIEPVAL WOOD at about midnight. The neighbourhood of NORTH BLUFFS was shelled frequently last night and this morning. 3500 Rounds were fired at Q 17 b 2.2. to Q 11 c 6.3. 2500 " " " " Q 18 b.	

2449 Wt. W14957/M90 750,000 1/16 J.B.C. & A. Forms/C.2118/12.

Army Form C. 2118.

WAR DIARY
or
~~INTELLIGENCE SUMMARY~~
(Erase heading not required.)

Instructions regarding War Diaries and Intelligence Summaries are contained in F. S. Regs., Part II. and the Staff Manual respectively. Title Pages will be prepared in manuscript.

Place	Date	Hour	Summary of Events and Information	Remarks and references to Appendices
AUTHUILLE	26/10/16		Enemy artillery active all day & night. A considerable amount of 77mm shells fell around AUTHUILLE & LANCASHIRE DUMP after dark.	
			2000 Rounds fired at Enemy's trench system N of R ANCRE.	
			2000 " " " Square R18b & HANSA RD.	
			Coy relieved by 116 M.G.Co. 2 Sections of 117 were left in under command of 116 Coy. Remainder of Coy proceeded to huts in Pioneer Road.	
PIONEER RD.	27/10/16		Coy H.Q. moved back to AUTHUILLE & took over line from 116. Two sections of 116 Coy remained in line under command of O.C. 117 Coy.	
AUTHUILLE.	28/10/16		Intermittent shelling on front & support lines throughout the day, heavier during the afternoon. Neighbourhood of AUTHUILLE was shelled during the night. Enemy M.Gs active at intervals during the night.	

Army Form C. 2118.

Instructions regarding War Diaries and Intelligence Summaries are contained in F. S. Regs., Part II. and the Staff Manual respectively. Title Pages will be prepared in manuscript.

WAR DIARY
or
~~INTELLIGENCE SUMMARY~~

(Erase heading not required.)

Place	Date	Hour	Summary of Events and Information	Remarks and references to Appendices
AUTHUILLE	28/10/16		2000 Rounds fired at Q.24 d 2.2. 2000 " " " Q.18 b trenches N. of St PIERRE DIVION.	
"	29/10/16		The Company (including 2 Sections of 116) was relieved by 48 M.G.Co. & proceed to rest Billets at SENLIS.	
SENLIS	30/10/16		Rest	
"	31/10/16		Rest.	

A Hall [illegible] Capt.

2449 Wt. W14957/M90 750,000 1/16 J.B.C. & A. Forms/C.2118/12.

117th Brigade.

39th Division.

117th BRIGADE MACHINE GUN COMPANY

NOVEMBER 1 9 1 6 :

117th Machine Gun Company Army Form C. 2118.

WAR DIARY
or
INTELLIGENCE SUMMARY
(Erase heading not required.)

Vol 7

Instructions regarding War Diaries and Intelligence Summaries are contained in F. S. Regs., Part II. and the Staff Manual respectively. Title Pages will be prepared in manuscript.

Place	Date	Hour	Summary of Events and Information	Remarks and references to Appendices
SENLIS	1/11/16		Rest.	
"	2/11/16		Rest.	
"	3/11/16		The company relieved the 118th M.G. Coy Coy H.Q established at AUTHUILLE BLUFFS.	
AUTHUILLE	4/11/16		Intermittent shelling throughout day + night heavier at about 10.0 p.m. 2000 Rounds fired at Enemy trenches N of R. ANCRE.	
"	5/11/16		Intermittent shelling 2000 Rounds fired at Enemy trenches N of R Ancre. The 117 Bde was relieved by the 116th 2 Sections of the 117 M.G. Coy left in under Command of O.C. 116 M.G. Co. The remainder of the Coy + Coy H.Q proceeded to SENLIS. Coy H.Q at Billet No 38 SENLIS.	
SENLIS	6/11/16		The 117th Bde relieved the 116th Bde + 2 Sections of 116 M.G.C. Coy H.Q at AUTHUILLE BLUFFS.	
AUTHUILLE	7/11/16		Very quiet on the whole some shelling round SCHWABEN REDOUBT during the afternoon. The N.C.O in charge of Gun at Point 16 Reports that 4 of our 18 pounder shells	

2449 Wt. W14957/M90 750,000 1/16 J.B.C. & A. Forms/C.2118/12.

Army Form C. 2118.

WAR DIARY
or
INTELLIGENCE SUMMARY
(Erase heading not required.)

Instructions regarding War Diaries and Intelligence Summaries are contained in F. S. Regs., Part II. and the Staff Manual respectively. Title Pages will be prepared in manuscript.

Place	Date	Hour	Summary of Events and Information	Remarks and references to Appendices
AUTHUILLE	7/11/16		hit this post at 11 am yesterday killing a Lewis Gunner	
			2000 Rounds fired at Q17 b 22	
			The Guns of the M.G. Co in ~~Prospect~~ PROSPECT TRENCH (N of ANCRE) fired	
			2000 Rounds at R13 c 8 1 traversing to R19 b 6.9	
			2000 " " R19 b 19 " " R14 c 05. 20	
			2000 " " R14 c 05 20 " " R19 b 4.9	
"	8/11/16		Trenches near POINT 16 shelled from 4 to 4.15 pm. & again from 5.45 to 6.15, but slightly more to the right.	
			Fairly quiet night	
			Heavy shelling N of R. ANCRE starting just after dark.	
			2500 Rounds were fired at Trenches N of River from Q24 c 91	
			5000 " " " " MILL TRENCH Q30 a 82	
"	"		The 117th Bde & M.G. Co were relieved by the 118 Bde & the G.C. & the Coy proceeded to rest billets in dugouts in PIONEER ROAD.	
PIONEER ROAD	9/11/16		Rest.	
" "	10/11/16		Rest	
" "	11/11/16		Coy. moved into Billets at Senlis.	

2449 Wt. W14957/M90 750,000 1/16 J.B.C. & A. Forms/C.2118/12.

Army Form C. 2118.

WAR DIARY
or
INTELLIGENCE SUMMARY
(Erase heading not required.)

Instructions regarding War Diaries and Intelligence Summaries are contained in F. S. Regs., Part II. and the Staff Manual respectively. Title Pages will be prepared in manuscript.

Place	Date	Hour	Summary of Events and Information	Remarks and references to Appendices
SENLIS	12/11/16		Coy moved into line as per attached operation order. Coy HQ at AUTHUILLE.	
AUTHUILLE	13/11/16		Coy co-operated in the attack + capture of ST PIERRE DIVION by the Brigade. (Casualties, 1. OR wounded) No 3 Section moved forward to ST PIERRE DIVION to assist in Consolidation	[illegible]
"	14/11/16		Brigade was relieved by Bde. + Coy proceeded (with remainder of Bde) to Billets at WARLOY. An enemy aeroplane dropped a bomb on the Camp at Warloy at 1.30 ~~[illegible]~~ am. 15/11/16	
WARLOY	15/11/16		~~Brigade~~ Coy moved to BEAUVAL (near DOULLENS) by road.	
BEAUVAL	16/11/16		Advance party left by train for BELLEZEELE.	
"	17/11/16	}	Coy moved by train to BELLEZELLE, one section going with each infantry Batt of the Bde.	
"	18/11/16	}		
BELLEZEELE	19/11/16		Rest	
"	20/11/16		Rest, Cleaning + checking equipment etc.	
"	21/11/16		As above	
"	22/11/16		Training	
"	23/11/16		Training. The Brigade was inspected by Gen Sir Aylmer Hunter Weston.	
"	24/11/16		Training	

2449 Wt. W14957/M90 750,000 1/16 J.B.C. & A. Forms/C.2118/12.

Army Form C. 2118.

Instructions regarding War Diaries and Intelligence Summaries are contained in F. S. Regs., Part II. and the Staff Manual respectively. Title Pages will be prepared in manuscript.

WAR DIARY
or
INTELLIGENCE SUMMARY

(Erase heading not required.)

Place	Date	Hour	Summary of Events and Information	Remarks and references to Appendices
BOLLEZEELE	25/11/16		Training.	
"	26/11/16		Training.	
"	27/11/16		Training.	
"	28/11/16		Training.	

A. Hall Capt.
[illegible] 117 M.G. Coy.

2449 Wt. W14957/M90 750,000 1/16 J.B.C. & A. Forms/C.2118/12.

No 6

OPERATION ORDER No. 3

by Captain A. Hall Hall, commanding 117 M.G. Coy.

1. A general attack will take place on Z day in accordance with orders explained verbally.

2. Action of 117 M.G. Coy.

No. 1 Section is allotted to the Divisional Reserve.
Nos. 2, 4 Sections will carry out barrage fire on the divisional front.
No. 3 Section is allotted to 16th N. & D. to consolidate ST PIERRE DIVION, [illegible] any other positions [illegible] by them. As there is not much [illegible] of a counter attack this section must be very alert for targets N. of the ANCRE.
One gun of No. 2 Section will cover the advance of 16th NOTTS & DERBY from MILL road, on their left flank.

3(a) Orders for No. 1 Section
They will keep touch with O.C. 17th NOTTS & DERBY.
On Y day this section will proceed to huts in PIONEER ROAD.

(b) Orders for No. 2 Section.
(1) One gun under good N.C.O. to cover the advance of 16th NOTTS & DERBY from the [illegible] of MILL ROAD as near the bridge as possible, [illegible] N of MILL ROAD.
It will fire [illegible] on the trench Q.24 & Q.8 – 26 from zero to zero + 25 and keep a good look out for [illegible] on the ground to the right of this trench over which the 16th NOTTS & DERBY will advance.
It must be remembered that our other troops will be coming down the hill from the direction of SCHWABEN REDOUBT.
This gun will remain in position.
(2) The other 3 guns will act in accordance with Brigade Order No. 89 but barrage lines will be as for group [illegible].

(c) Orders for No. 3 Section.
They will be under orders of O.C. 16th NOTTS & DERBY who will issue orders as to time of advance and position of assembly.
They will be attached to this battalion for hot meals, etc. during the operations.
On Y day they will proceed to NORTH BLUFFS.

(d) Orders for No. 4 Section.
The four guns will act in accordance with Brigade Order No. 89 but barrage lines will be as for group A. [illegible] first 5 of R 19 a 00.

(e) Orders for Transport
A B & C limbers for Nos 2, 3 and 4 Sections will be parked at W16 a 88 at zero + 2 hours with the transport of 17th NOTTS & DERBY and 17th KINGS ROYAL RIFLES, ready to move at [illegible] hours notice.
All other transport will be at present transport lines ready to move at [illegible] hours notice from zero.

4. Quarter Master's Stores and Company Office will remain at MARTINSART.

5 Packs and blankets will be stored at MARTINSART.
Haversacks will be carried on the back and waterproof sheets rolled.
One day's rations will be carried in addition to iron rations.

6. Movements on Y day.
[illegible] a.m. Nos 2, 3 and 4 Sections
[illegible] a.m. No. 1 Section and H.Q. (Cook cart and [illegible])
Packs and blankets and surplus kit will be stacked in the huts [illegible] handed up by No. 1 Section and transported to Quartermaster's Stores.

No 7

OPERATION ORDER No 3

by Captain A. Hall Hall, commanding 117 M.G. Coy

1. A general attack will take place on Z day in accordance with orders explained verbally.

2. Action of 117 M.G. Coy
No 1 Section [illegible] allotted to the Divisional Reserve
No 2 & 4 Sections will carry out barrage fire on the divisional front.
No 3 Section is allotted to 16th N & D. to consolidate ST PIERRE DIVION
[illegible] any other positions taken by them. As there is not much [illegible] of a counter attack this section must be very alert for targets N. of the ANCRE.
One gun of No 3 Section will cover the advance of 16th NOTTS & DERBY from MILL road, on their left flank.

3 (a) Orders for No 1 Section
They will keep touch with O.C. 17th NOTTS & DERBY.
On Y [illegible] this section will proceed to huts in PIONEER ROAD.

(b) Orders [illegible] No 2 Section.
(1) One gun under good N.C.O. to cover the advance of [illegible] NOTTS & DERBY from the [illegible] at MILL ROAD as near the bridge as possible, [illegible] M of MILL ROAD.
It will fire [illegible] on the trench [illegible] [illegible] zero + 25 and keep a good look out for other [illegible] on the ground to the right of this trench over which the 16th NOTTS & DERBY will advance.
It must be remembered that our other troops will be [illegible] from the direction of SCHWABEN REDOUBT.
This gun will remain in position.
(2) The other 3 guns will act in accordance with Brigade Orders No 87 but barrage lines [illegible]

(c) Orders for No 3 Section.
They will be under orders of O.C. 16th NOTTS & DERBY who will issue orders as to time of advance and position of assembly.
They will be attached to this battalion for hot meals, etc., during the operations.
On Y day they will proceed to NORTH BLUFFS.

(d) Orders for No 4 Section.
The four guns will act in accordance with Brigade Order [illegible] but barrage lines will be as for group A. [illegible] fire S. of R 19 a 00.

(e) Orders for Transport
[illegible] limbers for Nos 2, 3 and 4 Sections will [illegible] at W 16 c 88 at zero + 2 hours with the transport of [illegible] NOTTS & DERBY and of [illegible] KINGS ROYAL RIFLES, ready to move at [illegible] notice.
All other transport will be at present transport lines ready to move at [illegible] hours notice from zero.

4. Quarter Master's Stores and Company Office will remain at MARTINSART.

5. Packs and blankets will be stored at MARTINSART.
Haversacks will be carried on the back and waterproof sheets rolled [illegible]
[illegible] rations will be carried in addition to iron rations.

6. Movements on Y day.
9 a.m. of No 2, 3 and 4 Sections
11 a.m. of No 1 Section and H.Q. (Cook cart and G.S.)
Packs and blankets and surplus kit will be stacked in the [illegible] by No 1 Section and transported to Quartermaster's [illegible].

SECRET. Copy No. 5.

117th INFANTRY BRIGADEORDER No. 89.

31.10.1916.

Reference: 1/10000 BEAUMONT, 57D. S.E. 1 and 2, parts of.

1. Reference 117th Infantry Brigade Order No.85, dated 27/10/1916, para. 5(b).

The programme described in para 3 below will be carried out by the 117th Machine Gun Company (less one section, Divisional Reserve, and one section under orders of O.C., 16th Notts & Derby Regiment) on "Z" day.

2. The Gun Groups will be in their positions with their Guns and S.A.A. by 2 p.m. on "Y" day, and all Guns for barrage fire will be carefully laid during the hours of daylight on "Y" day.

3. The Guns will fire as follows, and adhere strictly to their programmes:-

GROUP "A" (4 Guns with fire positions at Q.30.b.3.3.) Q.24 b.5 8

Programme: (a) From ZERO to ZERO plus 8 Guns will barrage on the Line Q.24.d.8.7 - Q.24.b.85.15 - STONY Trench - SERB Road.

(b) At ZERO plus 8 all guns of the Group will gradually switch Westwards to the Line St.PIERRE DIVION - MILL Trench - JUNCTION of HANSA Line and MILL Road (R.13.b.4.5) actually reaching this Line with their barrage at ZERO plus 15.

(c) Group will fire on this Line from ZERO plus 15 to ZERO plus 22. Fire will cease at ZERO plus 22.

(d) Group will remain in Gun positions (under cover) after ZERO plus 22, and await further orders.

GROUP "B" (3 Guns with fire positions at Q.29.b.5.8). Q.30 a.8.2

Programme: (a) From ZERO to ZERO plus 22 Guns will barrage on the Line St.PIERRE DIVION - MILL Trench - JUNCTION of HANSA Line and MILL Trench (R.13.b.4.5).

(b) At ZERO plus 22 Guns will cease fire, pack up and proceed by road via SOUTHERN CAUSEWAY to the Trench Railway Junction at the East side of the CAUSEWAY about Q.30.c.45.15, where they will await orders. The arrival at this point will be immediately notified to Brigade Headquarters.

GROUP "C" (One Gun with fire position at Q.24.a.5.0).

This Gun will fire using direct observation on the Trench running from Q.24.b.6.4 to Q.24.b.3.6 from ZERO to ZERO plus 25, or later if necessary, and will cover the advance of the 16th Notts & Derby Regiment.

This Gun will remain in position after the advance.

4. One Officer of the Machine Gun Company will be with each Group, and carefully supervise the firing of the Group. O.C., 117th Machine Gun Company, will be with Group "B".

5. Arrangements for the synchronisation of watches will be notified later. The very greatest care must be exercised in obtaining the exact synchronisation with the Officers in charge of each Group.

P.T.O.

6. Arrangements regarding the Forward Parking of Machine Gun Company Limbered Wagons will be notified later.

7. ACKNOWLEDGE.

W.E.Maxwell Captain,

31.10.1916. Brigade Major, 117th Infantry Brigade.

Copies issued at 8 pm to:-

No.1. 16th Notts & Derby Regt.
2. 117th Machine Gun Company.
3. ditto
4. ditto
5. ditto
6. 117th T.M.Battery.
7. H.Q's, 39th Division.
8. H.Q's, ditto
9. H.Q's, 116th Brigade.
10. H.Q's, 118th Brigade.
11. G.O.C.
12. B.M.
13. S.C.
14. War Diary.
15. War Diary.
16. Order file.

117th Brigade.

39th Division.

117th BRIGADE MACHINE GUN COMPANY

DECEMBER 1 9 1 6

Instructions regarding War Diaries and Intelligence Summaries are contained in F. S. Regs., Part II. and the Staff Manual respectively. Title pages will be prepared in manuscript.

WAR DIARY
or
INTELLIGENCE SUMMARY.
(Erase heading not required.)

Army Form C. 2118.

117 Vol 8

117 Machine Gun Co

Place	Date	Hour	Summary of Events and Information	Remarks and references to Appendices
BOLLEZEELE	1/12/16	-	Training	
"	2/12/16	-	do	
"	3/12/16	-	do	
"	4/12/16	-	do	
"	5/12/16	-	do	
"	6/12/16	-	The 117th Infantry Bde + MGCo inspected on the March by GENl SIR HERBERT PLUMER G.C.M.G., K.C.B., Commanding 2nd Army, as per 117 Infantry Brigade order No103 attached.	
"	7/12/16	-	Training	
"	8/12/16	-	The 117th Infantry Bde, + MGCo inspected by LIEUT GEN. SIR AYLMER HUNTER-WESTON G.C.B, D.S.O., as per 117 Infantry Brigade Order No104, attached.	
"	9/12/16	.	Training	
"	10/12/16	.	The Company marched from BOLLEZEELE to HERZEELE see 117 Bde Order No105	
HERZEELE	11/12/16	.	The Company marched from HERZEELE to POPERINGHE, see 117 Bde Order No105,	
POPERINGHE	12/12/16	.	The Company marched from POPERINGHE to the trenches, ~~[illegible]~~ (LEFT SECTOR) YPRES SALIENT) where it relieved the 113th MGCo (38th (Welsh) Division) Twelve guns being in the line + 4 in reserve at Coy H.Q. Company Headquarters	

Instructions regarding War Diaries and Intelligence Summaries are contained in F. S. Regs., Part II. and the Staff Manual respectively. Title pages will be prepared in manuscript.

WAR DIARY
or
INTELLIGENCE SUMMARY.
(Erase heading not required.)

Army Form C. 2118.

Place	Date	Hour	Summary of Events and Information	Remarks and references to Appendices
YPRES	12/12/16		established at WEST CANAL BANK DUGOUTS (C19c 4 5) [Sheet 28 NW 1/10,000] See 117. Infantry Bde Order No 106 d/11/12/16 attached	
"	13/12/16		Fairly quiet during the night. Enemy Machine Guns active at intervals.	
"	14/12/16		One enemy machine Gun fired short bursts throughout the night from East of O2 position (C13a 2.8.) Direction of fire could not be ascertained A Yellow Rocket bursting into 2 Red stars was observed at 7.0 pm coming from the GERMAN LINES from the direction of FARM 14. Two Red Lights at 5 minute intervals were also observed in approximately the same locality. The neighbourhood of C13a 2.4 was shelled with 77 mm. shells between 8.0 am & 9.30 am. WORK DONE: Ammunition belts & boxes cleaned & inspected. Dugouts & emplacements cleaned & repaired. New Dugout at X2 (C19a 1½ 3) commenced. Water pumped out of dugout at Y1 (C19b 1½ 8) & trenches cleaned. Rounds fired Nil.	
"	15/12/16		Enemy machine Guns active at intervals during night otherwise fairly quiet. The neighbourhood of N. ZWAANHOF FARM was shelled during	

Instructions regarding War Diaries and Intelligence Summaries are contained in F. S. Regs., Part II. and the Staff Manual respectively. Title pages will be prepared in manuscript.

WAR DIARY
or
INTELLIGENCE SUMMARY.
(Erase heading not required.)

Army Form C. 2118.

Place	Date	Hour	Summary of Events and Information	Remarks and references to Appendices
YPRES.	15/12/16		the day.	
			WORK DONE. Continued cleaning & repairing Emplacements. Work on dugout at X1 Continued. Trenches cleaned & Dugout at D3 baled out & repaired.	
			Rounds fired. Nil	
"	16/12/16		An enemy machine Gun fired at intervals during the night onto the ration tramway running from CANAL BANK to LANCASHIRE FARM. This firing came from the direction of CAESARS NOSE. Otherwise quiet during the night.	
			WORK DONE. Revetting Emplacement at N1. New flooring into dugout at D3. Excavating commenced for new Section HQ near L.D. Bridge. Repairing & partly rebuilding emplacement at O3. Steps built to open emplacement at O2. Ammunition cleaned.	
			Rounds fired. Nil	

2353 Wt. W2544/1454 700,000 5/15 D. D. & L. A.D.S.S./Forms/C. 2118.

Instructions regarding War Diaries and Intelligence Summaries are contained in F. S. Regs., Part II. and the Staff Manual respectively. Title pages will be prepared in manuscript.

WAR DIARY
or
INTELLIGENCE SUMMARY.
(Erase heading not required.)

Army Form C. 2118.

Place	Date	Hour	Summary of Events and Information	Remarks and references to Appendices
YPRES.	17/12/16	-	Enemy Machine Guns active at intervals during the night. The neighbourhood of Lancashire Farm was shelled with heavy TRENCH MORTARS between 2.45 + 3.30	p.m.
			Otherwise quiet.	
		-	WORK DONE Building of new LEFT SECTOR, SECTION No 2. continued. Revetting trenches, laying new duckboards, Building dugouts of new emplacement at O2. Cleaning + repairing emplacements. No 3 Section relieved No 4 Section in LANCASHIRE FARM Sector.	
			ROUNDS FIRED. TARGETS. FROM GUN AT	
			2000 PILCKEM CROSS ROADS. C2 c 9.9. Z1. B12 c 4.5	
			2000. RAILWAY EMBANKMENT from C1 d 0.4 to C1 d 5.7. Z1. do	
			2000. CAESARS AVENUE from C8 a 7.3 to C2 c 8.0. X2. C19 a 3.7.	
			2000 TRENCH RAILWAY from GALLWITZ FARM (C8 a 7.3) to MACKENSEN FARM (C8 c 5.7.) X2 do.	
			8000 Total.	
"	18/12/16		Occasional shells on LANCASHIRE FARM area. Enemy machine Guns were active	

2353 Wt. W2541/1454 700,000 5/15 D. D. & L. A.D.S.S./Forms/C. 2118.

Army Form C. 2118.

Instructions regarding War Diaries and Intelligence Summaries are contained in F. S. Regs., Part II. and the Staff Manual respectively. Title pages will be prepared in manuscript.

WAR DIARY
or
INTELLIGENCE SUMMARY.
(Erase heading not required.)

Place	Date	Hour	Summary of Events and Information	Remarks and references to Appendices
YPRES	18/12/16		during the night. otherwise very quiet.	
			WORK DONE Cleaning + refilling Belts. Continued work on new LEFT SECTOR section HQ. Cleaning + repairing dugouts.	
			Commenced building latrines at B1. Renewed sandbagging + repaired emplacement at Y1.	
			OPERATIONS	
			Rounds. — Targets. — From Gun at	
			1300. — Caledonian Avenue — X2 C19.a.3.7.	
			2500 — Trench railways in neighborhood of Hindenburg Farm. — -do-	
			2000 — Trench railways from C1c 8.9 to C2a Central — Z1 B12.c.4.5.	
			2000 — Pilckem Cross Roads — -do-	
"	19/12/16		About 2.0 pm yesterday afternoon about 15 77mm shells were fired on LEFT SECTOR Section HQ + neighborhood. Enemy Machine Guns were heard at intervals during the night. Otherwise fairly quiet.	

2353 Wt. W2541/1454 700,000 5/15 D. D. & L. A.D.S.S./Forms/C. 2118.

Army Form C. 2118.

WAR DIARY
or
INTELLIGENCE SUMMARY.
(*Erase heading not required.*)

Instructions regarding War Diaries and Intelligence Summaries are contained in F. S. Regs., Part II. and the Staff Manual respectively. Title pages will be prepared in manuscript.

Place	Date	Hour	Summary of Events and Information	Remarks and references to Appendices
YPRES	19/12/16		WORK DONE Improving & repairing dugouts & emplacements. Belt filling & ammunition cleaning for night firing. Revetting trenches by X1 Gun. Constructing baby elephant at No 1 Position. Excavating for Baby Elephant dugout at new position in FARGATE. Continuing work of new LEFT SECTOR Section HQ.	
			Operations	
			Rounds — TARGETS — From Gun at	
			1500. — RAILWAY EMBANKMENT from C1c9.2 to C1d6.9 — Z1. (B12 c4.5)	
			800. — Communication Trenches from C1d0.32 to CARIBOU TR. — do	
			2000 — Trench Railways from C2b0.7 to C2a3.3. — do	
			2000 — CAESARS AVENUE & surrounding trench railways from MACKENSEN FARM to C2c8.0. — X2 (C19a3.7)	
			2000 — Trench railways in neighbourhood of HINDENBURG FARM — do	
			8000.	

2353 Wt. W2544/1454 700,000 5/15 D. D. & L. A.D.S.S./Forms/C. 2118.

Instructions regarding War Diaries and Intelligence Summaries are contained in F. S. Regs., Part II. and the Staff Manual respectively. Title pages will be prepared in manuscript.

WAR DIARY
or
INTELLIGENCE SUMMARY.
(Erase heading not required.)

Army Form C. 2118.

Place	Date	Hour	Summary of Events and Information	Remarks and references to Appendices
YPRES	20/2/16		Slight Artillery activity in the neighborhood of LANCASHIRE FARM. Enemy Machine Guns active during the day & night. At 10pm two red lights were seen in the left Sector. They were followed by a slight bombardment.	
			WORK DONE Continued building LEFT SECTOR Section HQ. Filling & cleaning ammunition Belts for night firing.	
			Building Baby Elephant at D1.	
			Finished Latrine at D1.	
			Improving cleaning & repairing dugouts and Emplacements.	
			Continuing work on Dugout at FARGATE. No 1 Section Relieved by No 4 in LEFT SECTOR.	
			Operations.	
			Rounds — Targets — From Gun at	
			2000 — RAILWAY EMBANKMENT. — D1.	
			2000. — PILCKEM CROSS ROADS — do -	
			2000. — HINDENBURG FARM & trench railways in neighborhood — X2.	
			2000. — CAESARS AVENUE do do — do.	
			8000.	

2353 Wt. W2544/1454 700,000 5/15 D. D. & L. A.D.S.S./Forms/C. 2118.

Army Form C. 2118.

WAR DIARY
or
INTELLIGENCE SUMMARY.
(Erase heading not required.)

Instructions regarding War Diaries and Intelligence Summaries are contained in F. S. Regs., Part II. and the Staff Manual respectively. Title pages will be prepared in manuscript.

Place	Date	Hour	Summary of Events and Information	Remarks and references to Appendices
YPRES.	21/12/16		Intermittent shelling on the left sector during the day. Rifle Grenades fell near Gun at F4 (B12 d 8 8) during the morning. BRIELEN + neighbourhood were shelled during the morning. Enemy Machine Guns active during night.	
			WORK DONE. Completing latrine at F1. Cleaning + improving dugouts + emplacements. Cleaning + refilling Belts for night firing. Draining + duckboarding trenches near F1 + revetting parapets. Building + fixing screens for night firing.	
			OPERATIONS.	

Rounds.	Targets	From Gun at.
2000	PILCKEM CROSS ROADS.	21
2000	RAILWAY EMBANKMENT	-do-
2000	Trench Railways near HINDENBURG FARM	21
1000	" " " MACKENSEN + GALLWITZ.	-do-
1000	CAESARS AVENUE	do
8000		

Army Form C. 2118.

Instructions regarding War Diaries and Intelligence Summaries are contained in F. S. Regs., Part II. and the Staff Manual respectively. Title pages will be prepared in manuscript.

WAR DIARY
or
INTELLIGENCE SUMMARY.
(Erase heading not required.)

Place	Date	Hour	Summary of Events and Information	Remarks and references to Appendices
Ypres	22/12/16		Intermittent Enemy Artillery activity during the day. Enemy Machine Guns active during the night Work done. Cleaning & improving emplacements & dugouts & revetting trenches. Continuing dugout at D1 & draining. Building new emplacement at D4. Laying duckboards at Z1 Building new Left Sector Section HQ. Operations Rounds. — Targets — From Gun at 2000 — Trench railways between GALLWITZ & MACKENSEN FARMS — Z1 2000. — PILCKEM CROSS ROADS. — -do- 2000 — HINDENBURG FARM & trench railway neighborhood — X2 2000 — CAESARS AVENUE — -do	
"	23/12/16		Intermittent Enemy Artillery activity during day on the LEFT SECTOR. A few shells were dropped near Coy HQ between 2.0 & 2.30 pm. Enemy MGs were active during the night. Enemy opened a heavy bombardment between	

2353 Wt. W2544/1454 700,000 5/15 D. D. & L. A.D.S.S./Forms/C. 2118.

Army Form C. 2118.

Instructions regarding War Diaries and Intelligence Summaries are contained in F. S. Regs., Part II. and the Staff Manual respectively. Title pages will be prepared in manuscript.

WAR DIARY
or
INTELLIGENCE SUMMARY.
(Erase heading not required.)

Place	Date	Hour	Summary of Events and Information	Remarks and references to Appendices
YPRES.	23/12/16		2. 330 am. Emplacement + Gun blown up at F. No casualties, gun undamaged. Two dugouts blown in on RIGHT SECTOR. 2 Casualties. (1 OR Killed + 1 wounded) WORK DONE Baby Elephant built at P1. Clearing + repairing dugouts + emplacements. Revetting trenches fallen in at Z1. Completing dugout at D1. Continuing work at Left Sector Section H2.	
			Operations	
			Rounds — Targets. — From Gun at	
			2000. — PILCKEM CROSS ROADS — Z1	
			2000. — Trench Railways in C2a. — -do-	
			2000. — CAESARS AVENUE + trench Rylo — Z2	
			2000. — HINDENBURG FARM. + trench railways — do	
			8000.	
"	24/12/16		Fairly quiet during the morning. Fairly heavy bombardment on left sector between 2.0 + 4.0 from both sides. Enemy MGs, less active during the night.	

2353 Wt. W2541/1454 700,000 5/15 D. D. & L. A.D.S.S./Forms/C. 2118.

Army Form C. 2118.

Instructions regarding War Diaries and Intelligence Summaries are contained in F. S. Regs., Part II. and the Staff Manual respectively. Title pages will be prepared in manuscript.

WAR DIARY
or
INTELLIGENCE SUMMARY.

(Erase heading not required.)

Place	Date	Hour	Summary of Events and Information	Remarks and references to Appendices
YPRES	24.12.16	-	WORK DONE. New Emplacement Commenced at F1. Digging out collapsed trench at O3, & revetting. Cleaning emplacements etc & refilling Belts for night firing at X1 & X2. Building left sector HQ	
			OPERATIONS.	
			From — Targets — Rounds	
			X1 — PILCKEM CROSS ROADS — 1000	
			X2 — HINDENBURG FARM — 1000	
			2000	
			Little indirect firing, due to High wind which rendered it unsafe.	
	25.12.16		Intermittent Artillery Activity during the day. Very quiet during the night. Enemy M.G.s less active than usual.	
			Work done. Excavating for Baby Elephant at P1. Repairing trenches & emplacements. New alternative emplacement built at Y1	

2353 Wt. W2544/1454 700,000 5/15 D. D. & L. A.D.S.S./Forms/C. 2118.

Army Form C. 2118.

Instructions regarding War Diaries and Intelligence Summaries are contained in F. S. Regs., Part II. and the Staff Manual respectively. Title pages will be prepared in manuscript.

WAR DIARY
or
INTELLIGENCE SUMMARY.

(Erase heading not required.)

Place	Date	Hour	Summary of Events and Information	Remarks and references to Appendices
Ypres.	25.12.16		Operations	
			From — Targets — Rounds	
			C2 — CANE TRENCH. — 2000.	
			" — Trench Railways in C9b. — 2000.	
			Z1 — CANDLE TRENCH & trench hqs near — 2000.	
			" — CANCER TRENCH & CANCER AVE. — 2000.	
			8000	
"	26.12.16.		Fairly quiet during the day & night a little artillery activity between 9 & 10.30 pm Enemy MGs quiet.	
			WORK	
			Continued work on Left Sector Section H.Q. Low Baby Elephant at P1	
			Repairing emplacement at [illegible]. Cleaning & repairing emplacements. Building Baby Elephants, & repairing damage at Right Sector HQ.	

2353 Wt. W2544/1454 700,000 5/15 D. D. & L. A.D.S.S./Forms/C. 2118.

Instructions regarding War Diaries and Intelligence Summaries are contained in F. S. Regs., Part II. and the Staff Manual respectively. Title pages will be prepared in manuscript.

WAR DIARY
or
INTELLIGENCE SUMMARY.
(Erase heading not required.)

Army Form C. 2118.

Place	Date	Hour	Summary of Events and Information	Remarks and references to Appendices
Ypres.	26/12/16		Operations	
			From — Targets — Rounds	
			Z1 — CANDLE TRENCH from SAPEUR HOUSE to JOLIE FARM — 2000	
			" — PILCKEM CROSS ROADS — 2000	
			X2 — GOURNIER FARM + Trench Rly — 2000	
			" — CANE Trench from JOLIE to CANISTER — 2000	
			8000	
"	27/12/16		~~Work done~~ Day and night quiet except for Aerial Activity. About 4.30 pm enemy Artillery bombarded neighborhood of Z1 gun. Red Flare fell about 50 yds from Left Sector HQ towards front line about 9. pm. Enemy aeroplane observed to fall about 11.30 am within our lines.	
			Work done	
			Z1 Anti-aircraft emplacement partially finished	
			O2. ditto ditto	
			P. Revetting trench Erecting Baby dugout	

2353 Wt. W2544/1454 700,000 5/15 D. D. & L. A.D.S.S./Forms/C. 2118.

Army Form C. 2118.

WAR DIARY
or
INTELLIGENCE SUMMARY.
(*Erase heading not required.*)

Instructions regarding War Diaries and Intelligence Summaries are contained in F. S. Regs., Part II. and the Staff Manual respectively. Title pages will be prepared in manuscript.

Place	Date	Hour	Summary of Events and Information	Remarks and references to Appendices
Ypres	27.12.16		D3. New Emplacement built. Y1. New Dugout built. New Fargate Emplacement, Excavation for baby Elephant. X1. Duckboards raised, subsoil cleaned, disinfected & drained.	
			Operations.	
			From — Targets — Rounds	
			X2 — PILCKEM CROSS ROADS — 2000	
			" — ~~CANDLE~~ CANDLE Trench from SAPEUR HOUSE to JOLIE FARM. — 2000	
			Z1 — CANCER TR. & CANCER AVE — 2000	
			" — CANDLE TR, & trench lips — 2000	
			Total — 8000	
"	28.12.16		Opposite LANCASHIRE FARM, what sounds like a tram has been heard behind enemy lines, at 5.10 a.m. also great activity apparently in the manufacture of dugouts. In this neighborhood bursts of artillery fire throughout the night. Elsewhere all quiet.	

2353 Wt. W2544/1454 700,000 5/15 D. D. & L. A.D.S.S./Forms/C. 2118.

Army Form C. 2118.

WAR DIARY
or
INTELLIGENCE SUMMARY.
(Erase heading not required.)

Instructions regarding War Diaries and Intelligence Summaries are contained in F. S. Regs., Part II. and the Staff Manual respectively. Title pages will be prepared in manuscript.

Place	Date	Hour	Summary of Events and Information	Remarks and references to Appendices
Ypres.	28.12.16.		Work done.	
			Work continued on Baby Elephants, Left Sector HQ & general improvement of trenches & gun positions.	
			Operations.	
			From — Targets — Rounds	
			Z1 — Trench C.1.c.7.9 to Rly Cutting – Pallisade Farm — 2000.	
			" — " C.1.d.6.8 to Cannon Farm. — 2000.	
			X2 — Pilckem Cross Roads — 2000	
			" — Candle Trench from Sapeur Ho. to Jolie Farm — 2000	
			8000	
"	29/12/16	-	Intermittent Artillery activity all day fairly quiet night	
			Work done — Work continued on Baby Elephants Left Sector HQ. & general Cleaning & repairing emplacements.	
			Operations	
			Z1 — Trench C.1.c.7.9 to Railway Cutting — 2000	
			" — C.1.d.6.8 to Cannon Farm — 2000	

2353 Wt. W2544/1454 700,000 5/15 D. D. & L. A.D.S.S./Forms/C. 2118.

WAR DIARY
or
INTELLIGENCE SUMMARY.
(Erase heading not required.)

Army Form C. 2118.

Instructions regarding War Diaries and Intelligence Summaries are contained in F. S. Regs., Part II. and the Staff Manual respectively. Title pages will be prepared in manuscript.

Place	Date	Hour	Summary of Events and Information	Remarks and references to Appendices
Ypres	29/12/16		I 2 HINDENBURG FARM 2000	
			" CAESARS AVENUE 2000	
			8000	
"	30/12/16		Fairly quiet all day & night. A little Artillery activity near LANCASHIRE FARM.	
			Work done Work continued on Dugouts etc, & general cleaning & improving.	
"			Operations	
			I 1. Trench C.I.C. 7.9 to PALLISADE FARM 2000	
			" CANNON FARM 2000	
			I C 2 HINDENBURG FARM 2000	
			MACKENSEN FARM 2000	
			8000	
"	31/12/16		Intermittent Artillery activity. Neighborhood of Left Sector Section H.Q. shelled during morning	

2353 Wt. W2541/1454 700,000 5/15 D. D. & L. A.D.S.S./Forms/C. 2118.

Instructions regarding War Diaries and Intelligence Summaries are contained in F. S. Regs., Part II. and the Staff Manual respectively. Title pages will be prepared in manuscript.

WAR DIARY
or
INTELLIGENCE SUMMARY.
(Erase heading not required.)

Army Form C. 2118.

Place	Date	Hour	Summary of Events and Information	Remarks and references to Appendices
Ypres	7/12/16		Work Continued on Dugouts, Emplacements etc.	
			Operations	
			Z1 Trench C1 c 7 9 to PALLISADE FARM	2000
			" C1 d 4 6 8 to CANNON FARM	2000
			X2 CAESARS FARM & Trench Rds near	2000
			" CAESARS AVENUE	2000
				8000

H. O. Rees Lieut
for OC 117 M.G. Coy.

2353 Wt. W2544/1454 700,000 5/15 D. D. & L. A.D.S.S./Forms/C. 2118.

Copy No. 4

117th INFANTRY BRIGADE ORDER No. 103.

5.12.1916.

Reference: 1/40,000 Map of France, Sheet 27.

1. General Sir Herbert Plumer, G.C.M.G., K.C.B., Commanding Second Army, will inspect the 117th Infantry Brigade on the March tomorrow, WEDNESDAY, December 6th., in accordance with the attached March Table

2. The Brigade Starting Point, at 9.40 a.m., is the Road Junction at A.24.d.8.5.

   The Divisional Starting Point, at 10 a.m., is the Forge in B.19.d.

3. (a) Dress will be Marching Order (Packs) and Steel Helmets.

   (b) Parade will be as strong as possible, and Parade States will be handed to the Brigade Major at the Brigade Starting Point at 9.35 a.m.

   (c) Transport, fully loaded, (less Baggage Waggons) will march in rear of each Unit. Dinners will be cooked in the Field Kitchens on the march.

   (d) Attention is drawn to Sect.25, Field Service Regs., Part 1, regarding distances behind Units.

4. The Army Commander will be about 100 yards S.W. of the Mill, in G.12.A. at 10.35 a.m.

5. Watches will be synchronised at 9.30 a.m. at the Brigade Starting Point (A.24.d.8.5.) An Officer from each Unit will attend for this purpose.

6. ACKNOWLEDGE.

W.E. Maxwell, Captain,
Brigade Major, 117th Infantry Brigade.

5.12.1916.

Copies issued at 8 p.m. to:-

No. 1. 16th Notts & Derby Regt.
2. 17th K.R.R.Corps.
3. 16th Rifle Brigade.
4. 117th Machine Gun Coy.
5. 117th Trench Mortar Battery.
6. H.Q's, 39th Division.
7. H.Q's, 39th Division.
8. G.O.C.
9. B.M.
10. S.C.
11. Brigade Sigs.Officer.
12. Brigade Bombing Officer.
13. War Diary.
14. War Diary.
15. Order file.

MARCH TABLE to accompany 117th INFANTRY BRIGADE ORDER No. 103.

Unit.	Time head of Unit to pass Brigade Starting Point.	Route to be taken to Brigade Starting Point.	Route for March.	Remarks.
117th Infantry Brigade Headquarters.	9.40 a.m.	--	FORGE in B.19.d. - MILL in G.12.A - Road Junction at G.11.d.7.1 - VOLKERINC - KHOVE - MERCKEGHEM - BOLLEZEELE.	
16th Notts & Derby Regiment.	9.43 a.m.	Via LEWERCKERVOIT - Road Junction G.5.a.4.9 - BOLLEZEELE.		
17th K.R.R.Corps.	9.48 a.m.	Via BOLLEZEELE.		
16th Rifle Brigade.	9.53 a.m.	--		
117th Machine Gun Company.	9.58 a.m.	Via BOLLEZEELE.		
117th Trench Mortar Battery.	10.1 a.m.			

REAR PARTY of 1 N.C.O. and 6 men will be found by the 17th K.R.R.CORPS.

The FIRST HALT will be ordered from the head of the Column: subsequent halts will be at the usual 10 minutes to clock hour.

Copy No...4.

117th INFANTRY BRIGADE ORDER No.104.

Ref:- 1/20,000 Sheet 27 N.W. 6.12.1916.

1. Reference this Office B.M./297 of the 4th instant, Lieut.General Sir Aylmer Hunter-Weston, K.C.B.,D.S.O., Commanding the VIII Corps, will inspect the 117th Infantry Brigade on FRIDAY, December 8th.,1916, in accordance with the attached Programme.

2. (a) Battalions will be formed up in close column by the right, in accordance with the attached plan, facing the entrance to the field in which they are parading, and will receive the Corps Commander with a General Salute when he arrives within 25 yards of the Battalion. Companies should be sized. Those men of Headquarter Companies not shewn in War Establishment will parade with their Companies.

   (b) The 117th Machine Gun Company, and the 117th Light Trench Mortar Battery, will parade fully equipped with full establishment of ammunition, ready for action at short notice.

   (c) Lewis Guns will be drawn up to go in rear of each Battalion.

   (d) First Line Transport, fully loaded, will be formed up for inspection in rear of each Battalion, and will leave the field as soon as it had been inspected.

   (e) After the Inspection of each Battalion close order drill will be carried out.

   (f) Officers and mens billets and messes will be inspected on the conclusion of each Unit.

   (g) All ranks will be in marching order, packs and steel helmets, carrying the full amount of ammunition, 120 rounds per man, unless otherwise laid down. Leather Jerkins will not be worn.

---

3. ACKNOWLEDGE.

W. E. Maxwell Captain,

6.12.1916. Brigade Major, 117th Infantry Brigade.

Copies issued to:-

No.1.16th Notts & Derby Regt.
2.17th K.R.R.Corps.
3.16th Rifle Brigade.
4.117th Machine Gun Coy.
5.117th Trench Mortar Battery.
6. H.Q's.,39th Division.
7. H.Q's.,39th Division.
8. G.O.C.
9. B.M.
10. S.C.
11 & 12. War Diary.
13. Order file.

Programme for Inspection of 117th Infantry Brigade
by
LIEUT. GENERAL SIR AYLMER HUNTER-WESTON, K.C.B., D.S.O.,
Commanding VIII Corps
on
8th December, 1916.

---

10 a.m.	Meet G.O.C., 39th Division, and Brigadier General Commanding 117th Infantry Brigade at Cross Roads B.19.b.2.0. Inspection of 16th Rifle Brigade in field at B.19.c.7.8,
10.30 a.m.	Close Order Drill by 16th Rifle Brigade.
10.35 a.m.	Inspection of billets and messes at BOLLEZEELE,
11.5 a.m.	Inspection of 117th Machine Gun Company in field at A.29.b.4.0.
11.10 a.m.	Inspection of 117th Light Trench Mortar Battery in field at A.29.b.4.0.
11.15 a.m.	Motor to MERCKEGHEM.
11.25 a.m.	Inspect 17th K.R.R.Corps in field at A.22.c.4.2.
11.55 a.m.	Close Order Drill by 17th K.R.R.Corps.
12 noon.	Inspection of billets and messes in MERCKEGHEM.
12.30 p.m.	Motor to VOLKERINCKHOVE.
12.35 p.m.	Inspect 16th Notts & Derby Regiment in field at G.15.a.2.5.
1.10 p.m.	Close Order Drill by 16th Notts & Derby Regiment.

CEREMONIAL

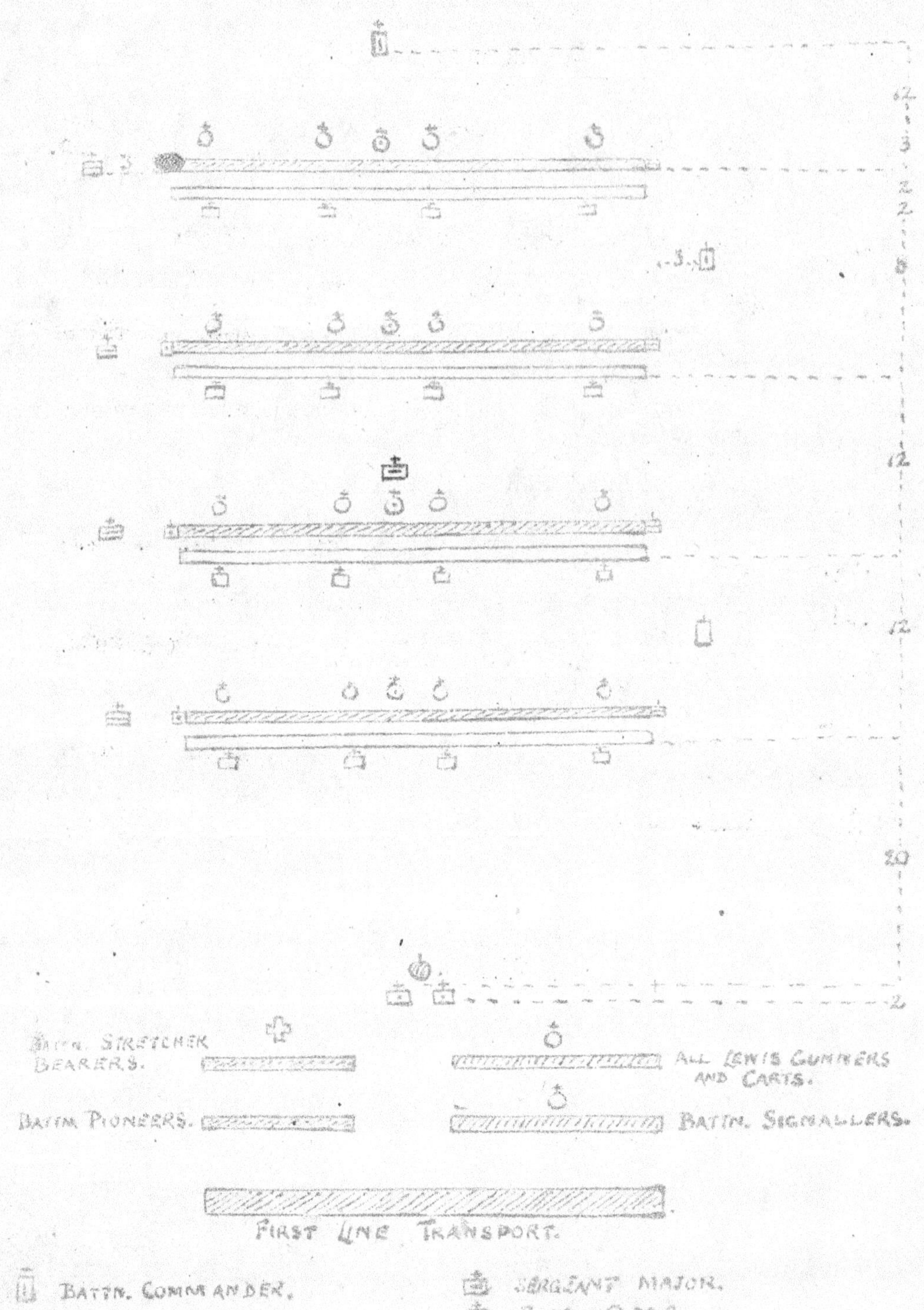

Battn. Commander.

Senior Major.

Adjutant.

Company Commander.

" 2nd in Command.

Platoon Commander.

Quartermaster.

Sergeant Major.

Battn. Q.M.S.

" Armourer Sergt.

Coy. Sergt. Major.

Coy. Q.M.S.

Platoon Sergt.

M.O.

SECRET.   Copy No. 5

117th INFANTRY BRIGADE ORDER No. 105.

Reference: Sheets 27 and 28.   9.12.1916.

1. (a) The 39th Division will relieve the 38th Division (Welsh) commencing on the 11th December.

   (b) The 117th Infantry Brigade will relieve the 113th Brigade on the 13th and 14th December.

   (c) The moves from present area will be in accordance with the attached Tables "A" and "B". Personnel only will proceed by train.

2. (a) The 17th Notts & Derby Regiment will remain at TATINGHEM until relieved by a Battalion of the 38th Division.

   (b) The 1/1st Cambridgeshire Regiment will be attached to the 117th Infantry Brigade until the 17th Notts & Derby Regiment rejoin the Brigade.

3. (a) Advance Parties of 1 Officer and 20 Other Ranks each from 16th Notts & Derby Regiment, and 16th Rifle Brigade, will proceed to POPERINGHE on the 10th. They will report to Headquarters, 116th Brigade, and will be rationed from there from the 11th instant inclusive.

   Buses for these parties will be at Brigade Headquarters at 9 a.m. on the 10th.

   (b) Advance Party of 1 Officer and 20 Other Ranks, from the 17th K.R.R.Corps, will proceed to POPERINGHE by the first train on the 11th. They will draw rations for the 12th from the 116th Brigade.

   (c) See below.

4. The following Motor Lorries have been applied for to assist in the removal of Quarter Masters' Stores:-

Each Battalion	... ...	Four.
117th Machine Gun Coy) 117th T.Mortar Bty.)	...	One.
117th Inf.Bde H.Q's.	...	One.

5. Units will send to Brigade Headquarters by 12 noon tomorrow, the 10th., an inventory in duplicate of all billet stores which will be left behind on vacating present billets.

6. The First Line Transport of each Unit will draw rations from WORMHOUDT STATION for its Unit for the following day as it passes through that place.
   Lewis Gun Detachments, and the 117th Machine Gun Company and 117th Trench Mortar Battery, will do the same.

7. 117th Infantry Brigade Headquarters will close at BOLLEZEELE at 11 a.m. on the 12th December, reopening on arrival in POPERINGHE.

8. ACKNOWLEDGE.

B.T. Maxwell
Captain,
9.12.1916.   Brigade Major, 117th Infantry Brigade.

O.N.

(c) Advance Party of 1 Officer, 3 Other Ranks, from 117th Machine Gun Coy., 1 Other Rank from each Battn.Lewis Gun Detachment, 1 Other Ranks from 117th Trench Mortar Bty., will parade at Brigade H.Q's at 8.45 a.m., the 10th., under an Officer to be detailed by 117th Machine Gun Coy., and will proceed by the bus referred to in 3(a) above, to fix billets in HERZEELE. On arrival at HERZEELE the Officer will report to O.C., 39th Divisional Supply Column for particulars as to accommodation.

P.T.O.

Copies issued at 8.15 p.m. to:-

No.1. 16th Notts & Derby Regt.
2. 17th, ditto
3. 17th K.R.R.Corps.
4. 16th Rifle Brigade.
5. 117th Machine Gun Coy.
6. 117th Trench Mortar Bty.
7. H.Q's, 39th Division.
8. ditto
9. H.Q's, 116th Brigade.
10. H.Q's, 118th Brigade.
11. H.Q's, 113th Brigade.
12. 1/1st Cambs. Regt.
13. No.3 Coy. Train.
14. Comdt., 39th Divl. Schools.
15. S.O.C.
16. B.M.
17. S.C.
18. Bde Signals Officer.
19. War Diary.
20. War Diary.
21. Order file.

T A B L E "A" to accompany 117th INFANTRY BRIGADE ORDER No. 105.

Unit.	DECEMBER 11th.			DECEMBER 12th.			DECEMBER 13th.		
	From.	To.	Remarks.	From.	To.	Remarks.	From.	To.	Remarks.
16th Notts & Derby Regt.	BOLLEZEELE Station.	Cheesemarket Stn, POPERINGHE to billet in POPERINGHE.	Go in two trains. 1st:11.30 a.m. 2nd:11.40	POPERINGHE.	Support Centre Section.	Train from G.8.b. at 4 p.m.	Support Centre Section.	Trenches.	--
17th K.R.R.C.	Remains in present billets.			BOLLEZEELE Station.	Cheesemarket Stn, Poperinghe to billet in Poperinghe	By trains. 1st:11 am. 2nd:11.10. 3rd:11.20.	Billets, POPERINGHE.	Support Centre Section.	Trains from G.8.b., 4 p.m.
16th Rfe. Bde.	BOLLEZEELE Station.	Cheesemarket Sn, POPERINGHE to billet in POPERINGHE.	By trains. 1st:11 am 2nd:11.10. 3rd:11.20	POPERINGHE.	Support Centre Section.	Train from G.8.b. 4 p.m.	Support Centre Section.	Trenches.	--
117th Bde. H.Q's.	Remains in present billets.			BOLLEZEELE Station.	Cheesemarket S. POPERINGHE, to billet in POPERINGHE.	By Train 11.20 am.	Billets, POPERINGHE.	Support Centre Section.	Train from G.8.b. 4 p.m.
1/1st Cambs. Regt. (attd. 117th Inf. Bde.	--	--	--	--	--	--	ELVERDINGHE & L.Works.	ditto	March Route.

NOTE: 1. Each Train on Metre Gauge (BOLLEZEELE to POPERINGHE) will take 250 All Ranks, and each train on ~~Brugxxx~~ Broad Gauge (POPERINGHE Eastwards) 1200 All Ranks.

2. Exact location of Battalions in Support Centre Section will be notified later.

3. Further Orders will be issued regarding all moves for December 13th.

T A B L E "B" to accompany 117th INFANTRY BRIGADE ORDER No. 104, shewing movements of 117th MACHINE GUN Coy., 117th TRENCH MORTAR Battery, Battalion Transport and Animals, Battalion Lewis Gun Teams and Handcarts.

Unit.	DECEMBER 10th.			DECEMBER 11th.		
	From.	To.	Remarks.	From.	To	Remarks.
117th Machine Gun Coy.	BOLLEZEELE.	Billets, HERZEELE.	March Route via ESQUELBECQ and WORMHOUDT.	HERZEELE.	Billets, POPERINGHE.	March Route. Order of March as on 10th. Leave HERZEELE 10 a.m.
117th Trench Mortar Bty.	BOLLEZEELE.	ditto.	As for 117th Machine Gun Coy.	HERZEELE.	ditto	ditto
16th Notts & Derby Lewis Guns Teams.	BOLLEZEELE.	ditto	As for 117th Machine Gun Coy.	HERZEELE.	ditto	ditto
16th Rifle Brigade Lewis Gun & Teams.	BOLLEZEELE.	ditto.	As for 117th Machine Gun Coy.	HERZEELE.	ditto	ditto
17th K.R.R.Corps Lewis Guns & Teams.	--	--	--	MERCKEGHEM.	HERZEELE.	March Route via ESQUELBECQ & WORMHOUDT to be clear of BOLLEZEELE by 11 a.m.
16th Notts & Derby Transport.	--	--	--	BOLLEZEELE.	POPERINGHE.	March Route See NOTE 2 overleaf.
17th K.R.R.Corps Transport.	--	--	--	--	--	
16th Rif.Bde.Tranport.	--	--	--	BOLLEZEELE.	POPERINGHE.	March Route. See NOTE 2 overleaf.
117th Bde.H.Q's Transport.	--	--	--	BOLLEZEELE.	POPERINGHE.	ditto

Movements on December 12th and 13th shewn overleaf.

Unit.	DECEMBER 12th.			DECEMBER 13th.		
	From.	To	Remarks.	From.	To.	Remarks.
117th Machine Gun Coy.	POPERINGHE.	Support Centre Section.	March Route.	Support Centre Section.	Trenches.	--
117th Trench Mortar Bty.	ditto	ditto	ditto	ditto	ditto.	--
16th Notts & Derby Lewis Guns & Teams.	ditto	ditto	ditto	ditto	ditto	--
16th Rifle Brigade Lewis Guns & Teams.	ditto	ditto	ditto	ditto	ditto	--
17th K.R.R.Corps Lewis Guns & Teams.	HERZEELE.	POPERINGHE.	March Route via ESQUELBECQ & WORMHOUDT to be clear of HERZEELE by 10 a.m.	POPERINGHE.	Support Centre Section.	March Route.
16th Notts & Derby Transport.	POPERINGHE.	Support Centre Section.	March Route.	--	--	--
17th K.R.R.Corps Transport.	MERCKEGHEM.	POPERINGHE.	March Route, leave MERCKEGHEM at 7 a.m.	--	--	--
16th Rifle Brigade Transport.	POPERINGHE	Support Centre Section.	March Route.	--	--	--
117th Bde H.Q's Transport.	POPERINGHE.	ditto	March Route.	--	--	--

NOTE: 1. Units marching to HERZEELE on December 10th will march in order:-117th Machine Gun Coy., 117th Trench Mortar Bty., Lewis Guns 16th Notts & Derby Regt., Lewis Guns 16th Rifle Brigade. Head of column to pass Brigade Headquarters at 10 a.m. Column to be under Command of Captain H.R.STEVENS, M.C.

2. Transport of 16th Notts & Derby Regt., and 16th Rifle Brigade, in this order will be clear of BOLLEZEELE by 7 a.m. on the 11th. Senior Transport Officer to command Column.

3. Transport of 17th K.R.R.Corps and 117th Brigade Headquarters in this order will be clear of BOLLEZEELE by 7 a.m. on the 12th. Transport Officer, 17th K.R.R.Corps, to command Column.

4. More detailed Orders regarding the Moves on the 12th and 13th will be issued later.

SECRET.

Copy No. 5...

AMENDMENT to 117th INFANTRY BRIGADE ORDER No. 105

10..2.1916.

Reference Move TABLE "B".

1. 117th Brigade Headquarters Transport.

The Moves detailed for December 11th. will take place on December 12th., and those detailed for December 12th. will take place on December 13th.

2. 17th K.R.R.Corps Transport.

Insert for DECEMBER 13th:-

"Move from POPERINGHE to SUPPORT CENTRE SECTION".

3. Acknowledge.

[signature], Captain,

10.12.1916

Brigade Major, 117th Infantry Brigade.

Copies issued to all recipients of 117th Infantry Brigade Order No. 105.

SECRET. Copy No. 5

Further AMENDMENTS to 117th Infantry Brigade Order No. 105.

10.12.1916.

TABLE "A".

16th Notts & Derby Regiment. DECEMBER 11th., Column 3.

For 11.30 a.m. substitute:- "12.29 arrive 15.16".

For 11.40 a.m. substitute:- "12.39 arrive 15.26".

DECEMBER 12th., Column 3.

For 4 p.m. substitute "4.30 p.m."

16th Rifle Brigade. DECEMBER 11th., Column 3.
Insert "two" between "by" and "trains".
For "11 a.m." substitute "11.59 arrive 15.00".
For "11.10" substitute "12.19 arrive 15.06".
Delete "3rd: 11.20".

DECEMBER 12th., Column 3.
For "4 p.m." substitute "4.30 p.m."

17th K.R.R.Corps. DECEMBER 12th., Column 3.
Insert "two" between "by" and "trains".
For "11 a.m." substitute "12.19 arrive 15.06".
For "11.10" substitute "12.29 arrive 15.16".
Delete "3rd: 11.20".

117th Brigade H.Q's. DECEMBER 12th., Column 3.
For "11.20 a.m." substitute "12.29 arrive 15.16".

NOTE 1. For "Each train on Metre Gauge (BOLLEZEELE to POPERINGHE) will take 250 All Ranks" substitute:-

"Accommodation of trains on Metre Gauge Railway (BOLLEZEELE to POPERINGHE) will be as follows:-

Dec.11th.	11.59	...	350 All Ranks.
	12.19	...	250 ditto
	12.29	...	250 ditto
	12.39	...	250 ditto
Dec.12th.	12.19	...	275 All Ranks.
	12.29	...	250 ditto "

NOTE: Attention is drawn to para.2 of 39th Divisional Instructions, 39/1285/A, dated 9.12.1916. Troops must arrive at Entraining Station at least half an hour before train departs.

ACKNOWLEDGE.

D.A. Coles Capt. for Captain,

10.12.1916. Brigade Major, 117th Infantry Brigade.

Copies issued to all recipients of 117th Infantry Brigade Order No.105.

SECRET. Copy No. 5.

117th INFANTRY BRIGADE ORDER No. 106.

11.12.1916.

Reference: Sheets 27 and 28.

1. With reference to and in continuation of 117th Infantry Brigade Order No.105. The following more detailed orders are issued regarding the relief of the 113th Infantry Brigade in the Centre Section on the 12th and 13th December.

2. (a) The relief will be carried out in accordance with the attached tables and Line will be taken over exactly as held by the 113th Infantry Brigade. All details not mentioned in this Order will be arranged direct between Commanding Officers.

   (b) Details of Work in progress, Defence Schemes, etc., will be taken over as usual.

3. No formed bodies will move East of ELVERDINGHE - VLAMERTINGHE Road before 4.15 p.m., while holding the Centre Section.

4. The transport of all Battalions, and the 117th Brigade Transport, will be at A.14.b.8.8.

   The transport of the 117th Machine Gun Company will be at A.22.d.8.2.

   Transport Officers, and Quartermasters, will reconnoitre these Lines while their Units are in POPERINGHE, and will take over Lines as under:-

   16th Notts & Derby Regiment from 14th Royal ~~xxxx~~ Welsh Fusiliers.
   1/1st Cambs Regiment from 13th Royal Welsh Fusiliers.
   17th K.R.R.Corps from 15th Royal Welsh Fusiliers.
   16th Rifle Brigade from 16th Royal Welsh Fusiliers.

5. The following Posts (garrison of 1 N.C.O. and 3 men each) will be taken over by the 16th Rifle Brigade on the 12th December, viz:-

   Post G.8. (A.1.B.)
   Post G.7. (A.2.c.)
   Post G.6. (A.8.B.)
   Post G.5.N. (A.9.D.4.6.)

   A Guide from each Post will be in the Square, POPERINGHE, by the CHURCH, at 11 a.m. on the 12th., for the purpose of guiding the new garrisons to their posts.

6. Three buses are being arranged for to be in the Square, POPERINGHE, at 8.30 a.m., 12th December.

   One each is allotted to 16th Notts & Derby Regt., and 16th Rifle Bde.
   One is allotted to 117th Machine Gun Coy., and 117th Trench Mortar Battery.

   The above Units will arrange to send Advance Parties of Officer & N.C.O's to reconnoitre the Front and Reserve Lines, and await the arrival of their Units.

   Advance Parties of the 117th Machine Gun Coy., and 117th Trench Mortar Battery, should include No. 1's for each Gun Position.

7. The Command of the Centre Section will pass to G.O.C., 117th Infantry Brigade, as soon as relief is complete on the 13th December.

   Brigade Report Centre will close at POPERINGHE at 3.30 p.m. on the 13th, and reopen at WEST CANAL BANK DUGOUTS (C.19.c.4.3) at 7 p.m.

8. ACKNOWLEDGE.

W.E. Maxwell Captain,
Brigade Major, 117th Infantry Brigade.

11.12.1916.

Copies issued at 9 a.m. to all recipients of 117th Infantry Brigade Order No.105.

R E L I E F   T A B L E   to accompany 117th INFANTRY BRIGADE ORDER No.106.

Date.	Unit.	Arrive Asylum Stn., YPRES.	Relieving.	Advance Party Guides.	Platoon, Coy., and Section Guides.	Destination.	Remarks.
Dec. 12th.	16th Notts & Derby Regiment.	5.30 p.m.	16th R.Welsh Fusiliers.	113th Bde H.Q's. 9.30 a.m.	Meet Battn at the Asylum Stn., YPRES. 5.30 p.m.	Battn in Right Reserve.	
ditto	16th Rifle Brigade.	ditto	14th R.Welsh Fusiliers.	ditto	ditto	Battn in Left Reserve.	
ditto	117th Machine Gun Company.	--	113th Machine Gun Company.	ditto	ESSEX Fm/Cross Rds, C.25.a.2.8. 5.30 p.m.	Trenches.	To leave POPERINGHE by March Route in time to arrive at ESSEX Fm Cross Roads at 5.30 pm. Column under Command of Captain STEVENS, M.C.
ditto	117th Trench Mortar Battery.	--	113th Trench Mortar Battery.	ditto	ditto	Trenches.	

NOTE: 1. Lewis Gun Teams will leave POPERINGHE at 1 p.m., and proceed by March Route under Senior Lewis Gun Officer to ASYLUM Station, YPRES, and await arrival of Battalions. March with Battalions from YPRES to destination.

2. Transport with Officers' Kits, and Dixies, etc., required for the trenches, will proceed with above party.

PTO

RELIEF TABLE TO ACCOMPANY 117th INFANTRY BRIGADE ORDER No.106.

Date.	Unit.	Arrives ASYLUM Stn., YPRES.	Relieving.	Advance Party Guides.	Platoon and Coy. Guides.	Destination.	Remarks.
Dec. 13th.	16th Notts & Derby Regt.	--	13th R.Welsh Fusiliers.	As arranged.	As arranged.	Right Battalion Centre Section.	Relief to be complete by 8 pm. See FOOTNOTE 2.
ditto	17th K.R.R. Corps.	5 p.m.	16th Notts & Derby Regt.	As arranged.	Platoon & Coy Guides from 16th Notts & Dby to meet Battn at Asylum Stn, YPRES 5pm	Battalion in Right Reserve.	To be in position by 8 p.m.
ditto	16th Rifle Brigade.	--	15th R.Welsh Fusiliers.	As arranged.	As arranged.	Left Battalion Centre Section.	Relief to be complete by 8 p.m. See FOOTNOTE 2.
ditto	1/1st Cambs. Regiment.	--	16th Rifle Brigade.	--	As arranged.	Battalion in Left Reserve.	To be in position by 8pm. Route from L.Work to be reconnoitred on morning of 13th, also position of Companies.
ditto	117th Bde H.Q's.	5 p.m.	113th Bde H.Q's.	--	1 Guide from 113th Bde. H.Q's.	West Canal Bank Dug-outs. C.19.c.4.3.	Report Centre will open at 7 p.m.

NOTE:- 1. NOTES 1 and 2 on Table for the 12th will hold good for the 17th K.R.R.Corps.

2. As far as possible the relief by the 16th Notts & Derby Regiment, and 16th Rifle Brigade, will take place by day.

SECRET.

DISPOSITION TABLE to accompany 117th INFANTRY BRIGADE ORDER No.106.

Brigade Headquarters:	West Canal Bank - C.19.c.4.3.
Right Front Battalion: 16th Notts & Derby Regiment.	Battn Headquarters - Canal Bank East, C.19.c.5.5. 3 Companies in front line from C.14.d.3½.6½. to C.13.B.75.35 (exclusive). 1 Company - Lancashire Farm.
Left Front Battalion: 16th Rifle Brigade.	Battn Headquarters - Canal Bank West, C.13.c.1.2. 3 Companies in front line from C.13.b.75.35 (inclusive) to Canal Bank. 1 Company - Colne Valley, Fargate, and Butts 19, 20, 22.
Right Reserve Battalion: 17th K.R.R.Corps.	Battn Headquarters - Trois Tours B.28.Central. 1 Company, Canal Bank East, N. of Bridge 4. 1 Company, Canal Bank West, S. of Bridge 4. 2 Companies, Trois Tours.
Left Reserve Battalion: 1/1st Cambs Regiment.	Battn Headquarters - Canal Bank West, C.19.a.1.6. 4 Companies, Canal Bank West.
117th Machine Gun Coy:	Headquarters - Canal Bank West, C.19.c.2½.6.
117th Trench Mortar Bty:	Headquarters - Canal Bank East, C.19.c.2½.8½.

Instructions regarding War Diaries and Intelligence Summaries are contained in F. S. Regs., Part II. and the Staff Manual respectively. Title pages will be prepared in manuscript.

Army Form C. 2118.

WAR DIARY
or
~~INTELLIGENCE SUMMARY.~~
(Erase heading not required.)

117th Machine Gun Coy.

Vol 9

Place	Date	Hour	Summary of Events and Information	Remarks and references to Appendices
	1917			
Ypres	2 Jan 17		There was intermittent Artillery activity all day. especially on LEFT SECTOR Red & Green light were sent up opposite LEFT SECTOR at 5.30 & 7.30 pm. Work done. Baby Elephant dugout built at Coy H.Q. Emplacements & dugouts at D3 drained. General cleaning & repairs at all emplacements & dugouts. Operations from — Targets — Rounds X I1 (B12 c1.3) — CANDLE TRENCH. — 2000 " — PILCKEM CROSS ROADS. — 2000 Z2 (C19 a 3.7) — CAESARS AVENUE — 2000 " — Trench Railways between MACKENSEN and GALLWITZ FARMS — 2000 Total — 8000	
"	3 Jany		Very quiet all day. Enemy MGs active at intervals during night. Work done Continued work on new H.Q. for LEFT SECTOR.	

2353 Wt. W2544/1454 700,000 5/15 D. D. & L. A.D.S.S./Forms/C. 2118.

Army Form C. 2118.

WAR DIARY
or
INTELLIGENCE SUMMARY.
(Erase heading not required.)

Instructions regarding War Diaries and Intelligence Summaries are contained in F. S. Regs., Part II. and the Staff Manual respectively. Title pages will be prepared in manuscript.

117 COY. M. G. C.

Place	Date	Hour	Summary of Events and Information	Remarks and references to Appendices
Ypres.	3 Jan		Completed Baby Elephant at Coy HQ. Cleaning & general repairs & maintenance at all emplacements & dugouts. Filling & cleaning belts & ammunition for night firing.	
			Operations. Indirect fire from	
			Z2 (C19a3.7) on HINDENBURG FARM & Trench Railway in C19c	2000
			" CAESARS AVENUE & trench Rys near	2000.
			Z1 (B12 C4.3) Trench Railways in C2a	2000
			" PILCKEM CROSS ROADS.	2000
				8000
"	4 Jan		FARGATE was shelled about 12.0 noon. The neighborhood of Coy HQ was shelled between 1.15 pm & 2.30 pm. Very quiet during night.	
			Work done.	
			Continued work on new Section HQ in left Sector. Building protected look outs for Sentries. Repairing Dugout at Z1. Improving positions at P4, O2, & P1. Cleaning amm:	

2353 Wt. W2544/1454 700,000 5/15 D. D. & L. A.D.S.S./Forms/C. 2118.

Instructions regarding War Diaries and Intelligence Summaries are contained in F. S. Regs., Part II. and the Staff Manual respectively. Title pages will be prepared in manuscript.

WAR DIARY
or
INTELLIGENCE SUMMARY.
(Erase heading not required.)

Army Form C. 2118.

117 COY. M. G. C.

Place	Date	Hour	Summary of Events and Information	Remarks and references to Appendices
Ypres.	4 Jan		+ refilling Belts for night firing. Cleaning dugouts and general maintenance at all positions.	
			Operations. Indirect fire.	
			From Z1 on Trench C1 c.7.9 to Railway Cutting PALLISADE FARM 2000	
			" " Trench C1 d 6 3 " CANNON FARM. 2000	
			X2 " Trench Railways between GALLWITZ and MACKENSEN FARMS. 2000	
			X2 " Trench Railways between MACKENSEN and HINDENBURG FARMS. 2000	
			8000	
"	5 Jan		Bombardment by Enemy of our front line between 8.30 + 9.30 pm Night quiet.	
			Work done. At Z1 N1, Y1, Z3 work in hand, Continues Cleaning + draining emplacements. Reserve ammunition cleaned. New Emplacement begun at N1. Work continued at Left Sector HQ. General work on baby	

2353 Wt. W2541/1454 700,000 5/15 D. D. & L. A.D.S.S./Forms/C. 2118.

Instructions regarding War Diaries and Intelligence Summaries are contained in F. S. Regs., Part II. and the Staff Manual respectively. Title pages will be prepared in manuscript.

WAR DIARY
or
~~INTELLIGENCE SUMMARY.~~
(Erase heading not required.)

Army Form C. 2118.

117 COY. M. G. C.

Place	Date	Hour	Summary of Events and Information	Remarks and references to Appendices
Ypres	5 Jan		Elephants, Cleaning trenches, emplacements at other Gun positions. Operations: From 21 — Pilckem Cross Roads ,2000 Trench Rlys in C2a ,2000 X2 — Caesars Avenue & Trench Rlys near ,2000 " — Trench Rlys near Hindenburg Farm 2000.	
"	6 Jan		Two Enemy planes over our lines at 1.45 pm. Occasional bursts of M.G. fire during night. Work done. Continuing work on Left Sector HQ. Sandbagging baby Elephant in front of Coy HQ. Reerection of baby Elephant at N1 & work on alternative emplacement. Reserve belts cleaned, General improvement & draining of trenches near Gun position & X1. Operations From X2 Cactus Avenue from C7 Central to C1d 1.4. 4000 " 21 Trench Railway Mauser Cot to Hindenburg Farm 4000	

2353 Wt. W2544/1454 700,000 5/15 D. D. & L. A.D.S.S./Forms/C. 2118.

Instructions regarding War Diaries and Intelligence Summaries are contained in F. S. Regs., Part II. and the Staff Manual respectively. Title pages will be prepared in manuscript.

WAR DIARY
or
~~INTELLIGENCE~~ SUMMARY.
(Erase heading not required.)

Army Form C. 2118.

117 COY. M.G.C.

Place	Date	Hour	Summary of Events and Information	Remarks and references to Appendices
Ypres	7.1.17		LANCASHIRE FARM shelled about 12.30 pm. Enemy bombarded front line near LANCASHIRE FARM between 3 + 3.30 am. Red + green lights seen on left about 8.30 pm. Workdone. 2 Dugouts on E bank of Canal redrained + improved Reserve Belts cleaned. Revolver practise carried on. Operations from X2. CACTUS AVENUE from Cy Central C.i.d.14 4000	
"	8.1.17		Night quiet Workdone. Sandbagging + covering Elephant at Section HQ. Upkeep of Emplacements. Cartage of material for protected look outs. Operations X2. CACTUS AVENUE from Cy Central to C.i.d.14 4000	
"	9.1.17		Occasional shelling + bursts of MG fire on left Workdone Work continued on Left Section HQ. Construction of baby	

2353 Wt. W2544/1454 700,000 5/15 D. D. & L. A.D.S.S./Forms/C. 2118.

Instructions regarding War Diaries and Intelligence Summaries are contained in F. S. Regs., Part II. and the Staff Manual respectively. Title pages will be prepared in manuscript.

WAR DIARY
or
~~INTELLIGENCE~~ SUMMARY.
(Erase heading not required.)

Army Form C. 2118.

117 COY. M.G.C.

Place	Date	Hour	Summary of Events and Information	Remarks and references to Appendices
Cuinchy	9/1/17		Elephant at R4. Upkeep of trenches. Operations. X2. CACTUS AVENUE 4000.	
"	10/1/17		N1 + D1 positions shelled about 8.30 am + 2.30 pm. West Canal Banks just S of HARGATE shelled at intervals during the day. Work done. Work continued at Section H.Q. Repairing D. Out at Coy H.Q. which collapsed. Commenced Protected Lookout at O3. Repairs to trench + Emplacement at J. Draining + repairs. Operations. From X2 GALLWITZ FARM 2500 Rounds.	
"	11/1/17		Heavy bombardment on Right, beyond our Sector between 4 + 6 pm, also Trench Mortar activity along our Front. Work done. Repair of fallen trench at X2. Protected lookout at	

Instructions regarding War Diaries and Intelligence Summaries are contained in F. S. Regs., Part II. and the Staff Manual respectively. Title pages will be prepared in manuscript.

WAR DIARY
or
INTELLIGENCE SUMMARY.
(Erase heading not required.)

Army Form C. 2118.

117 COY. M.G.C.

Place	Date	Hour	Summary of Events and Information	Remarks and references to Appendices
Ypres.	11/1/17		OS Continued. Materials for Concrete wall of Elephant Carried up. Drainage and General repairs. Bomb Throwing practised. Operations Nil.	
"	12/1/17		Quiet day & night. Upkeep & repair of trenches. Cleaning & repairing belts. Operations. From X2 JOLLY FARM & French Railways near 350.	
"	13/1/17		Short Bombardment by our artillery on Right. Generally Quiet. Work done Upkeep of emplacements & trenches. Draining etc. Cleaning & drying belts. Revolver practice. Operations — Nil.	
"	14/1/17		Bombardment on Right between 5 & 6 pm. Drainage & repair of Gun positions.	

2353 Wt. W2544/1454 700,000 5/15 D. D. & L. A.D.S.S./Forms/C. 2118.

Instructions regarding War Diaries and Intelligence Summaries are contained in F. S. Regs., Part II. and the Staff Manual respectively. Title pages will be prepared in manuscript.

WAR DIARY

or

~~INTELLIGENCE SUMMARY.~~

(Erase heading not required.)

Army Form C. 2118.

117 COY. M. G. C.

Place	Date	Hour	Summary of Events and Information	Remarks and references to Appendices
Ypres	15/1/17		Artillery activity from 11 am to 4 pm on Right Sector. Quiet day & night on Left Sector.	
			Work done. Clearing EALING TRENCH. Carrying U frames & revetting frames for repair of trenches at	
			X1 + X2. Drainage & general repairs.	
			Operations.	
			From gun at X2. JOLIE FARM & adjacent trenches & tramways 4500.	
"	16/1/17		The company was relieved by 118 M.G.Co. & proceeded to Camp G. BRANDHOEK. as per 117 Inf Bde Order & amendments attached	Bde order 1916 attached
BRANDHOEK	17/1/17		Rest.	
			9 Guns placed in position at the RAMPARTS, Ypres.	
"	18/1/17		Training	
"	19/1/17		Training	
"	20/1/17		Training. No 3. + 4 Sections relieved Nos 1 + 2 at Ramparts YPRES.	
"	21/1/17		Training	
"	22/1/17		Training	
"	23/1/17		Training	
+	~~24/1/17~~			

2353 Wt. W2541/1454 700,000 5/15 D. D. & L. A.D.S.S./Forms/C. 2118.

Army Form C. 2118.

Instructions regarding War Diaries and Intelligence Summaries are contained in F. S. Regs., Part II. and the Staff Manual respectively. Title pages will be prepared in manuscript.

WAR DIARY
or
INTELLIGENCE SUMMARY.
(Erase heading not required.)

117 COY, M. G. C

Place	Date	Hour	Summary of Events and Information	Remarks and references to Appendices
BRANDHOEK	24/11/17		The coy relieved 118th Machine Gun Coy in the WIELTJE Sector. Coy HQ at CANAL BANK near "Kaaie".	
WIELTJE	25/11/17		Very quiet morning. Intermittent artillery activity during evening. Otherwise quiet.	
"	26/11/17		Fairly quiet day except for intermittent shelling. Enemy's MGs active during night. Gas alarm received at 8.15 pm. Work done. Ammunition cleaned. Dugouts & Emplacements cleaned & repaired.	
"	27/11/17		Intermittent shelling by both sides during day. A German aeroplane brought down in German Lines at 4.15 pm. S.O.S. went up on Extreme Left at 6 pm.	
"	28/11/17		Enemy MGs active during night. Otherwise quiet. Work done. Pumping at John St & LIVERPOOL Trenches. Operations from CONGREEVE WALK to CAMBRAI DRIVE, CANDY LANE & [illegible] Rds 4000 Rds.	

2353 Wt. W2541/1454 700,000 5/15 D. D. & L. A.D.S.S./Forms/C. 2118.

Instructions regarding War Diaries and Intelligence Summaries are contained in F. S. Regs., Part II. and the Staff Manual respectively. Title pages will be prepared in manuscript.

WAR DIARY
or
~~INTELLIGENCE SUMMARY.~~
(Erase heading not required.)

Army Form C. 2118.

117 COY. M.G.C.

Place	Date	Hour	Summary of Events and Information	Remarks and references to Appendices
WIELTJE	29.1.17		Enemy MGs active round WELTJE FARM & BROWSE FARM. New Gun position at C28.4 improved. Maintenance & General repairs operations. Indirect fire on Trenches N.W. of MOUSETRAP FARM – 4000 Rounds.	
"	30.1.17		Quiet during day & night. Enemy MGs active at night. General Cleaning, repairs & maintenance of Emplacements & dugouts. Reserve belts cleaned and inspected. 3000 Rounds fired on Trench Railways & Communication trenches N.W. of MOUSETRAP FARM.	
"	31.1.17		Enemy Artillery Active throughout day & night. Also his MGs active at night. General cleaning & repair of Emplacements & dugouts. Reserve belts cleaned, refilled & dried. Guns & revolvers cleaning.	

2353 Wt. W2544/1454 700,000 5/15 D. D. & L. A.D.S.S./Forms/C. 2118.

Army Form C. 2118.

Instructions regarding War Diaries and Intelligence Summaries are contained in F. S. Regs., Part II. and the Staff Manual respectively. Title pages will be prepared in manuscript.

WAR DIARY
or
~~INTELLIGENCE SUMMARY.~~
(Erase heading not required.)

117 COY. M. G. C.

Place	Date	Hour	Summary of Events and Information	Remarks and references to Appendices
WIELTJE	31/1/17		Operations. (Indirect fire)	
			6000 rounds on trenches near OSKAR FARM.	
			6000 " " " NW. of MOUSETRAP FARM & JASPER FARM	

A. O. Lees. Lieut.
for O.C. 117 M.G. Coy

2353 Wt. W2544/1454 700,000 5/15 D. D. & L. A.D.S.S./Forms/C. 2118.

SECRET.   Copy....6.....

117th INFANTRY BRIGADE ORDER No. 116.

Reference Paper Trench Paper map and Sheet 28.N.W.

1. The 117th Infantry Brigade will be relieved by the 113th Infantry Brigade in the CENTRE Section between the 13th and 15th January,1917, in accordance with attached Table "A". All details of relief not mentioned in these orders will be arranged direct between Commanding Officers concerned. Wherever possible, Trench garrisons in the Front Line will be relieved by day, starting at 2 p.m.

   During the day however, great care is to be taken that parties larger than a section do not move up or down communication trenches at a time, and large intervals are to be maintained between all parties.

2. Units will on relief hand over the following:-

   (a) Defence Schemes, maps and plans and all information regarding their Sub-Section.

   (b) A statement of work (both defence and administrative) under construction and proposed.

   (c) All Trench and Camp stores which are normally handed over from one unit to another.

   (d) All R.E. material and tools in excess of Units authorised establishment.

3. Guns of 113th Machine Gun Coy and 113th Light Trench Mortar Battery and a portion of the personnel will arrive on night of Jany 14/15th, and will be accomodated by their respective " opposite numbers" for the night.

4. Orders for the move of Transport Lines and Qr.Mr.Stores will be issued by the Staff Captain, who will also arrange for two limbers to be placed at the disposal of 117th Light Trench Mortar Battery for the move.

5. Completion of each relief will be wired to Brigade Hd.Qrs in Code. Reports on arrival in Billets will also be sent in.

6. 117th Infantry Brigade Report Centre will close on CANAL BANK.C.19.c.4.3. at 8.30 p. . on 14th instant, re-opening at Camp C (A.30.a.) at the same hour.

7. ACKNOWLEDGE.

[signature] Captain.
a/Brigade Major 117th Infantry Bde.

10.1.1917.

Copies issued at 8 p.m. to :-

		15. G.O.C.
No.1. 16/Notts & Derby.R.	8. H.Q's. 39th Division.	16. B.M.
2. 17/Notts & Derby.R.	9. H.Q's. 39th do	17. S.C.
3. 17/K.R.Rif.C.	10.O.C.227th Field Coy.R.E.	18. B.S.O.
4. 16/Rifle Brigade.	11.H.Q's 116th Brigade.	19. B.B.O.
5. 117th M.G.Coy.	12. H.Q's118th Brigade.	20. War Diary.
6. 117th T.M.Battery.	13.H.Q's.113th Brigade.	21. War Diary.
7. O.C., Centre Group.R.A.	14. 39th Divl Signals.	22.Order File.

TABLE "A"

R E L I E F   T A B L E   TO ACCOMPANY 117th INFANTRY BRIGADE ORDER No. 116.

No.	Date.	Unit.	Relieved by.	Proceed to.	Platoon and other guides.	REMARKS.
1.	13/14th.	Rifle Bde: 16/~~Royal Welsh Fuslrs.~~ (Left Support)	16/Royal Welsh Fuslrs.	D.E.G. or P. Camp. To be notified later.	MARENGO Ho. 5.45.p.m.	To keep N.W. of the line POND COTTAGE -REIGERS BURG, on arrival in D.E.G. or P. Camp, in Divl Reserve to 39th Div. 16th Royal Welsh Fus become L support/to 117th Infy Bde.
2.	13/14th	16/Notts & Derby.R. (Right Support)	14/Royal Welsh Fuslrs.	ditto.	Guides for two Coys on Canal Bank only at W. end of Bridge 4 at 5 p.m.	To keep N.W. of the line POND COTTAGE - REIGERS BURG. On arrival in D.E.G. or P Camp, in Divl Reserve to 39th Divn, 14/Royal Welsh Fuslrs become R.Support Battn to 117th Bde,
3.	14/15th	16/Rifle Brigade.	From D. .C. or P. Camp.	A.B.C. or O Camp. (To be notified later)	-	On arrival in A.B.C. or O. Camp in Divl Reserve to 55th Division.
4.	14/15th.	16/Notts & Derby.R.	ditto.	ditto.	-	ditto.
5.	14/15th.	17/K.R.Rif.C. (Left Front Battn)	16/Royal Welsh Fuslrs.	ditto.	As arranged between C.Os concerned	Relief to commence at 2 p.m. and to be complete by 7.30.pm 17/K.R.Rif.C. will rendezvous in Field opposite Bn. Hd.Qrs & not move from there before 6 p.m.
6.	14/15th.	17/Notts & Derby.R. (Right Front Battn)	14/Royal Welsh Fuslrs.	ditto.	ditto.	Relief to commence at 2 p.m. & to be complete by 7.30.p.m. 17/N & D. will rendezvous in Field on ESSEX Road & not to move from there before 7 p.m.

P.T.O.

TABLE "A" Continued.

No.	Date.	Unit.	Relieved by.	Proceed to	Platoon & other guides.	REMARKS.
7	14/15th.	16/Royal Welsh Fuslrs. (Left Support Battn)	15/Royal Welsh Fuslrs.	- -	As arranged between C.Os concerned.	16/Royal Welsh Fuslrs will carry on with relief of Front Line, and will not await the arrival of 15/Royal Welsh Fuslrs.
8.	14/15th.	14/Royal Welsh Fuslrs.	13/Royal Welsh Fuslrs.	-	ditto.	14/Royal Welsh Fuslrs will carry on with relief of Front Line, and will not await the arrival of 13/Royal Welsh Fuslrs.
9.	14/15th.	117/Infantry Brigade Hd.Qrs.	113th Infantry Brigade Hd.Qrs	Camp. C. A.30.a.	-	-
10.	15/16th.	117th Machine GunCoy.	113th Machine Gun Coy.	Camp A.B.C. or O.	To be arranged between C.Os concerned.	Relief to be complete by 8 p.m.
	15/16th	117th L.T.M. Battery.	113th L.T.M. Battery.	ditto.	ditto.	ditto.

NOTE. Units will arrange to send on Billeting Parties to their respective Camps.

SECRET. Copy....5..

AMENDMENT TO 117th INFANTRY BRIGADE ORDER No. 116.

1. Reference 117th Infantry Brigade Order No. 116 and Table "A".

The following amendments will be made :-

	Heading.	
Item No. 1.	"Proceed to"	For D.E.G. or P. Camp. Substitute "G" Camp. (A.16.a.9.4.)
" No. 2.	"Proceed to"	For D.E.G. or P. Camp Substitute "P" Camp. (A.15.d.5.0.)
" No. 3(a)	"Relieved by"	For D.E.G. or P. Camp. Substitute "G" Camp.
(b)	"Proceed to"	For A.B.C. or O. Camp Substitute "O" Camp. (A.30.Central)
" No. 4(a)	"Relived by"	For D.E.G. or P. Camp. Substitute "P" Camp.
(b)	"Proceed to"	For A.B.C or O Camp. Substitute "C" Camp. (A.30.d.1.4.)
" No. 5	"Procedd to"	For A.B.C. or O. camp. Substitute "A" Camp. (H.1.d.7.9.)
" No. 6.	"Proceed to"	For A.B.C. or O. Camp. Substitute "B" Camp. (G.6.b.5.2.)
" No. 10 (117/M.G.Coy)	"Proceed to"	For A.B.C. or O. Camp. Substitute G.12.b.8.6. (Camp)
Item No. 10. (117/T.M.B)	"Proceed to"	For A.B.C. or O. Camp. Substitute "C" Camp.

O.H. Wilkinson Capt.
Captain.
Brigade Major 117th Infantry Bde.

11.1.1917.

No. 1. 16th Notts & Derby.R.
2. 17th Notts & Derby.R.
3. 17th K.R.Rif.C.
4. 16th Rifle Brigade.
5. 117th Machine Gun Coy.
6. 117th Trench Mortar Battery.
7. O.C., Centre Group, R.A.
8. H.Q's. 39th Division.
9. H.Q's 39th do
10. O.C., 227th Field Coy.R.E.
11. H.Q's 116th Brigade.

No. 12. H.Q's, 118th Brigade.
13. H.Q's. 113th Brigade.
14. 39th Divnl Signals.
15. G.O.C.
16. B.M.
17. S.C.
18. B.S.O.
19. B.B.C.
20. War Diary.
21. War Diary.
22. Order File.

Instructions regarding War Diaries and Intelligence Summaries are contained in F. S. Regs., Part II. and the Staff Manual respectively. Title pages will be prepared in manuscript.

WAR DIARY
or
INTELLIGENCE SUMMARY.
(Erase heading not required.)

117 M. Gun Coy

Army Form C. 2118.

Vol 10

Place	Date	Hour	Summary of Events and Information	Remarks and references to Appendices
WELTJE	1/2/17	—	Ypres was shelled in morning, and afternoon at intervals. Enemy Machine Guns active at night. Heavy bombardment on Right at 5.15 to 5.45 a.m.	
			Work done. Cleaning and repairs to all emplacements + dugouts. Spare parts and spare ammunition and belts cleaned.	
			Operations	
			6000 Rounds indirect fired on Trench Railway + communication trenches N.W. of MOUSETRAP FARM.	
"	2/2/17		Intermittent shelling all day and night. Enemy machine Guns active at night. Enemy aircraft also very active during day.	
			Work done. General cleaning + maintenance to emplacements + dugouts etc. Spare ammunition + belts cleaned.	
			Operations.	
			6000 Rounds indirect fired at Communication trenches + trench Railways N.W. of Mousetrap Farm.	

Instructions regarding War Diaries and Intelligence Summaries are contained in F. S. Regs., Part II. and the Staff Manual respectively. Title pages will be prepared in manuscript.

WAR DIARY
or
INTELLIGENCE SUMMARY.
(Erase heading not required.)

Army Form C. 2118.

Place	Date	Hour	Summary of Events and Information	Remarks and references to Appendices
WIELTJE	3/2/17		Fairly quiet day. The neighborhood of POTIJZE Chateau shelled during the afternoon.	
			Work done. General repairs & maintenance of Emplacements & dugouts. Reserve ammunition cleaned.	
			Operations. Nil	
			The 117th Machine Gun Coy was relieved in the WIELTJE Sector by the 118th Machine Gun Coy. It then proceeded to relieve the 116th Coy in RAILWAY Wood Sector, as per 117th Inf Bde Order No 120 attached.	117 Inf Bde Order No 120 attached.
Railway Wood.	4/2/17		Fairly quiet day. Enemy MGs active at night.	
			Work done General Cleaning & maintenance of dugouts & emplacements. Relief.	
			Operations Nil	
"	5/2/17		Our front lines heavily shelled with Trench Mortars during	

Army Form C. 2118.

Instructions regarding War Diaries and Intelligence Summaries are contained in F. S. Regs., Part II. and the Staff Manual respectively. Title pages will be prepared in manuscript.

WAR DIARY
or
~~INTELLIGENCE SUMMARY.~~
(Erase heading not required.)

Place	Date	Hour	Summary of Events and Information	Remarks and references to Appendices
[illegible]WAY WOOD	5/2/17		Q[illegible] morning & afternoon. Enemy M.G's active at night. Work done Cleaning & repairing Dugouts & emplacements, cleaning ammunition and reserve belts. Operations Nil.	
" "	6/2/17		Intermittent shelling during day. Enemy M.G's active at night. At 4.30 p.m. an enemy aeroplane dropped a light near DEER TR. This was followed by shelling of the neighbourhood. Work done. Emplacements cleaned and repaired. Ammunition belts cleaned, dried, etc. Dugout at DILLY FARM, pumped out. Operations. Nil	
"	7/2/17		Enemy Artillery & Trench Mortars active all day & Machine guns active at night.	

Instructions regarding War Diaries and Intelligence Summaries are contained in F. S. Regs., Part II. and the Staff Manual respectively. Title pages will be prepared in manuscript.

WAR DIARY
or
~~INTELLIGENCE SUMMARY.~~
(Erase heading not required.)

Army Form C. 2118.

Place	Date	Hour	Summary of Events and Information	Remarks and references to Appendices
RAILWAY WOOD.	7/2/17		Dugouts, Emplacements & trenches cleaned & repaired where necessary. Spare belts refilled and ammunition cleaned.	
			OPERATIONS.	
			2000 rounds at Dump at J1d 45.75	
			2000 " RAILWAY EMBKT I6d2.6 to I6d8.4.	
			2000 " Trenches near ZIEL HOUSE.	
			2000 " tramways near SIEBEN HOUSE.	
"	8/2/17		Enemy Artillery active during the day. The neighborhood of the Ecole was shelled between 1230 + 1.30 pm. Enemys Machine Guns active at night.	
			WORK DONE. Emplacements + dugouts cleaned and repaired. Belts filled and Ammunition cleaned.	
			OPERATIONS.	
			2000 Rounds at Trench railway from I12b6.6. to ZIEL HOUSE.	
			2000 " " RAILWAY EMBANKMENT I6.c	

2353 Wt. W2544/1454 700,000 5/15 D. D. & L. A.D.S.S./Forms/C. 2118.

Army Form C. 2118.

Instructions regarding War Diaries and Intelligence Summaries are contained in F. S. Regs., Part II. and the Staff Manual respectively. Title pages will be prepared in manuscript.

WAR DIARY
or
INTELLIGENCE SUMMARY.
(Erase heading not required.)

Place	Date	Hour	Summary of Events and Information	Remarks and references to Appendices
RAILWAY WOOD.	8.2.17.		2000. Rounds on Trenches & Tramway near SIEBEN HOUSE.	
			2000. " " Tramway from I18a 00.84. to CROSS ROADS I7d 90.25.	
"	9.2.17		Enemy artillery active all day. The neighborhood of the Ecole was shelled at various times during the day. Dugout of Gun team at B5 sustained a direct hit & all the team were injured. A fire was caused at MENIN GATE at 5.40 pm. by hostile shelling.	
			Emplacements dugouts etc cleaned and repaired. Belts refilled and ammunition cleaned	
			2000 rounds fired at RAILWAY EMBANKMENT.	
			2000 " " " Trench railway I7a 5.7. to I1d 4.5.	
"	10.2.17		Enemy artillery active all day, especially in Right Subsector. Machine Guns active at night. Enemy sent up a greater number of "Very" Lights than usual. The Flash of a machine Gun was observed about I11.b 90.85.	

2353 Wt. W2541/1454 700,000 5/15 D. D. & L. A.D.S.S./Forms/C. 2118.

Instructions regarding War Diaries and Intelligence Summaries are contained in F. S. Regs., Part II. and the Staff Manual respectively. Title pages will be prepared in manuscript.

WAR DIARY
or
~~INTELLIGENCE~~ SUMMARY.
(Erase heading not required.)

Army Form C. 2118.

Place	Date	Hour	Summary of Events and Information	Remarks and references to Appendices
RAILWAY WOOD.	10.2.17		New Latrine built at Left Sector H.Q. + latrine at X2 improved. Dugouts + Emplacements repaired where necessary + cleaned. Belts refilled, spare ammunition cleaned.	
			2000 Rounds fired at RAILWAY EMBANKMENT I6d.	
			2000 " " " Trench Railway (I12 b.6.6 to ZIEL HOUSE)	
			2000 " " " Tramways + road from J13 a. 05. to CLAPHAM JUNCTION.	
			2000 " " " Tramways in J13a.	
"	11.2.17		Artillery active during the day. The neighborhood of the Ecole was shelled in the morning and in the afternoon, very heavily between 5 + 6.30 pm. Also the MENIN + POTIJZE ROADS. His M.G's did not appear to be so active at night as usual. Enemy still sending up a great number of "Very" lights. Emplacements, Dugouts + Trenches cleaned and repaired. Continued work on latrines in Left SECTOR. Emergency emplacement in front of CORK COTS improved + Gun Platform built + ammunition carried there. Belts filled + ammunition cleaned.	

2353 Wt. W2544/1454 700,000 5/15 D. D. & L. A.D.S.S./Forms/C. 2118.

Instructions regarding War Diaries and Intelligence Summaries are contained in F. S. Regs., Part II. and the Staff Manual respectively. Title pages will be prepared in manuscript.

WAR DIARY
or
INTELLIGENCE SUMMARY.
(Erase heading not required.)

Army Form C. 2118.

Place	Date	Hour	Summary of Events and Information	Remarks and references to Appendices
RAILWAY WOOD	11.2.17		2000 Rounds fired at RAILWAY EMBKT I6d. 2000 " " " French Railways I12b 2000 " " " Trenches near ZIEL HOUSE. 2000 " " " Tramway from J13a.0.8.	
"	12.2.17		Fairly quiet during the day. Enemy artillery active at intervals. MGs active at night. Dugouts & emplacements cleaned & repaired. Ammunition cleaned & belts refilled. N.F. Screens made. 2000 Rounds fired on French Railways in I7a Central 2000 " " " Tramway from I12b0.6. to I7a a.b. 2000 " " " Tramway near SIEBEN HOUSE 2000 " " " Tramways in J13a.	
"	13/2/17		Enemy MGs active at night. Enemys artillery active all day especially about 12.30pm.	

2353 Wt. W2544/1454 700,000 5/15 D. D. & L. A.D.S.S./Forms/C. 2118.

Army Form C. 2118.

WAR DIARY
or
~~INTELLIGENCE SUMMARY.~~
(Erase heading not required.)

Instructions regarding War Diaries and Intelligence Summaries are contained in F. S. Regs., Part II. and the Staff Manual respectively. Title pages will be prepared in manuscript.

Place	Date	Hour	Summary of Events and Information	Remarks and references to Appendices
13/2/17 RAILWAY WOOD.	to 9 a.m. 13/2/17		**WORK DONE.** Emplacements, Dugouts & Trenches cleaned and repaired. Ammunition cleaned and belts filled. Night firing screens made. Positions prepared for forthcoming operation.	
			Operations	
			2000 Rounds fired at ZIEL HOUSE & trenches in neighborhood.	
			2000 " " " Tramways in J13a.	
			2000 " " " Dump in J6.b.8.6. (WILDE COTTAGE)	
			2000 " " " RAILWAY EMBANKMENT from I6d.a.6.b — I6.b.8.0.	
"	14/2/17		Enemy Artillery and trench mortars active during day. Enemy machine guns active at night.	
			The Coy cooperated in a raid by the 16th Rifle Brigade as per attached operation orders. (117 Inf Bde order No 124 & amendments. 117 MGCo O.O. No 20 & amendments).	
			Rockets bursting into a number of golden stars, were sent up by the enemy when our barrage started. Whilst barrage was on, a	

2353 Wt. W2544/1454 700,000 5/15 D. D. & L. A.D.S.S./Forms/C. 2118.

Army Form C. 2118.

*Instructions regarding War Diaries and Intelligence Summaries are contained in F. S. Regs., Part II. and the Staff Manual respectively. Title pages will be prepared in manuscript.

WAR DIARY
or
~~INTELLIGENCE SUMMARY.~~
(Erase heading not required.)

Place	Date	Hour	Summary of Events and Information	Remarks and references to Appendices
RAILWAY WOOD	14/2/17		rocket bursting into golden rain in the shape of a cone were sent up.	
			WORK DONE.	
			Emplacements, + dugouts, cleaned & repaired. Pumped etc.	
			Dugouts [illegible].	
			OPERATIONS. Barrage fire around area raided.	
			4000 Rounds [illegible] IBEX SUPPORT. 3500 CAMEROON SUPPORT.	
			3500 " " " IBEX LANE. 4000 CAMEROON AVENUE.	
			4000 " " " IBERIA RESERVE. 1500 CAMEROON RESERVE.	
			3500 " " " CAMEROON TRENCH. 4000 IBERIA AVENUE.	
"	15.2.17.		Enemy artillery active during day. The neighborhood of Coy HQ at ECOLE de BIENFAISANCE was shelled between 5- + 6.30 pm. Enemy MGs active at night.	
			WORK DONE	
			Dugouts and Emplacements cleaned and repaired. Belts filled ammunition cleaned. Pumps carried to GULLY FARM, + RIFLE FARM.	
			Operations	

2353 Wt. W2544/1454 700,000 5/15 D. D. & L. A.D.S.S./Forms/C. 2118.

Army Form C. 2118.

WAR DIARY
or
~~INTELLIGENCE SUMMARY.~~
(Erase heading not required.)

Instructions regarding War Diaries and Intelligence Summaries are contained in F. S. Regs., Part II. and the Staff Manual respectively. Title pages will be prepared in manuscript.

Place	Date	Hour	Summary of Events and Information	Remarks and references to Appendices
RAILWAY WOOD	5/2/17		2300 Rounds fired on Dump J 7 a 4.5. (ZIEL HOUSE)	
			2000 " " " Tramway from J 7 a 9 2 to WESTHOEK	
			1700 " " " RAILWAY EMBANKMENT from I 6 c 8 4	
			2000 " " " Dump J 7 a 9 3 to I 6 d 2 6	
	6/2/17		Enemy's Artillery and trench Mortars active during day. The neighborhood of ECOLE was shelled at 1.0 pm to midnight.	
			Emplacements & dugouts cleaned. Ammunition cleaned & shells refilled. Pumping at GULLY FARM.	
			1 pump taken to RITZE FARM.	
			2100 Rds at Dump J 7 a 9 3	
			1900 Tramway Junction J 7 a 77 75.	
			1500 Trench J 7 a 75. 50 to J 7 b 1.8	
			1500 Neighborhood of SIEBEN HOUSE.	
			1500 Dump at J 1 d 45.75	

Instructions regarding War Diaries and Intelligence Summaries are contained in F. S. Regs., Part II. and the Staff Manual respectively. Title pages will be prepared in manuscript.

WAR DIARY
or
INTELLIGENCE ~~SUMMARY~~.
(Erase heading not required.)

Army Form C. 2118.

Place	Date	Hour	Summary of Events and Information	Remarks and references to Appendices
RAILWAY WOOD.	17/2/17.		Fairly quiet during the day. Some trench mortar activity against RAILWAY WOOD. Machine guns active during night.	
			<u>Work done</u>	
			Emplacements & dugouts cleaned and repaired. Trench which had been blown in by T.M. at I11.3 repaired. Belts refilled and ammunition cleaned. S.A.A. carried to Right Sectn.	
			<u>Operations</u>	
			2000 Rounds fired at Trench Junction ~~[illegible]~~ J7a 05.85	
			2000 " " " Trench J7c 70 85 to J7 d 05 95.	
			1600 " " " Tramway I12 b66. to J7 a77	
			1600 " " " Railway Embkt from I6 c 84 to I6 d 2.6.	
"	18/2/17		Artillery active at intervals during day. Also Trench Mortars. The Ecole and [illegible] Wood was shelled at 4.30pm & 5.30pm. Machine Guns active at night.	
			<u>Work done</u>. Dugouts and emplacements cleaned and repaired. Pumping	

Army Form C. 2118.

Instructions regarding War Diaries and Intelligence Summaries are contained in F. S. Regs., Part II. and the Staff Manual respectively. Title pages will be prepared in manuscript.

WAR DIARY
or
INTELLIGENCE SUMMARY.
(Erase heading not required.)

Place	Date	Hour	Summary of Events and Information	Remarks and references to Appendices
RAILWAY WOOD	18/2/17		Dugouts etc., Bdes filled, and ammunition cleaned.	
			Operations	
			2000 Rounds fired at Dump J 1 d 45.75	
			1700 " " " Tramway I 7 a 4 1 to I [illegible]	
			1500 " " " Tramway J 13 a 55.90 to J 7 d 25.15.	
			1500 " " " Trench I 12 b 7.0 to J 7 a 3.1.	
			1800 " " " Dump J 7 a 4.5.	
" "	night of 18/19		The Coy was relieved by 165 M.G. Coy. After relief Coy proceeded to "S" Camp	
			as per attached order (107 Inf Bde order No 127.	
"S" CAMP	19/2/17		Rest & training	
	20/2/17		Training.	
	21/2/17		Training.	
	22/2/17		Training	
	23/2/17		Training	
	24/2/17		Training	
	25/2/17		Coy moved into Billets at the HOSPICE YPRES. Coy HQ at HOSPICE.	

2353 Wt. W2544/1454 700,000 5/15 D. D. & L. A.D.S.S./Forms/C. 2118.

Instructions regarding War Diaries and Intelligence Summaries are contained in F. S. Regs., Part II. and the Staff Manual respectively. Title pages will be prepared in manuscript.

WAR DIARY

or

~~INTELLIGENCE SUMMARY.~~

(Erase heading not required.)

Army Form C. 2118.

Place	Date	Hour	Summary of Events and Information	Remarks and references to Appendices
YPRES.	26/2/17		The company relieved the 68th M.G. Coy in the L ZILLEBEKE sector 9 guns in the line, 4 at ZILLEBEKE BUND & 3 in YPRES. Fairly quiet during day. YPRES shelled at intervals.	
"	27/2/17		Fairly quiet during day. Ypres shelled at intervals & also ZILLEBEKE. M.Gs active at night. Work done under R.E. supervision at GORDON HOUSE, YEOMANRY POST, RITZ ST, WELLINGTON CRES, ROSSLYN ST etc.	
"	28/2/17.		Fairly quiet day. Bombardment on Right about 10 pm. Gun at ROSSLYN St fired 750 Rounds on S.O.S. lines. M.Gs active at night. Work done under REs supervision at GORDON HOUSE, YEOMANRY POST, RITZ St WELLINGTON CRESCENT & ROSSLYN ST.	
			[illegible] Lieut for O.C. 67 M.G. Coy	

Copy No 8

SECRET

117 M.G. Co. Operation Order No. 20.

REFERENCE:-
ST. JULIEN Sheet 28 N. W. 1/10,000

Day of operation is referred to as 'Z' day

Intention (1) To co-operate in a raid on the enemy trenches.

Objectives of RAIDS (2) 'A' raid will have as its objectives:- Front German Line from I 5 b 6.6. to C 29 d. 4.0 German Support Line from I 5 b 75.45 to I 5 b 58.99. and will be carried out by 16th RIFLE BRIGADE.
'B' raid will have as its objectives:- C 29 a 53.60 to C 23 c 25.00 & German Support Line C 29 a 75.80 to C 23 c 53.07 and will be carried out by 1/1st HERTS. REGT.

ACTION OF 117 M. G. Co (3) Eight guns of 117 M. G. Coy. and four guns (attached) of 116 M. G. Coy. will cover the flanks of "A" raid with intense fire.

2.

Positions of Guns & targets will be as laid down in attached table. Guns will be in position at ZERO minus ONE hour.

No. 1 GROUP 4 GUNS — One Section of 116 M. G. Coy under LIEUT. PLATTS.

No. 2 GROUP 3 GUNS. — Two guns of No. 3 Section, these will be taken from ST. JAMES TRENCH & HAYMARKET positions, and one gun and team from No. 2 Section, this will come from HELL FIRE CORNER, under 2ND LT. RUTLEDGE.

No. 3 GROUP 3 GUNS — Three guns of No. 4 Section under LIEUT. BROOKE.

No. 4 GROUP 2 GUNS. — ONE gun from No. 1 Section. This will be reserve gun from the mine. One gun and team from No. 4 Section.

O's. C. No. 2 & 4 Sections will arrange for guns & teams as above to be attached to the Groups mentioned.

Guns taken from battle emplacements will return there immediately after the raid.

AMMUNITION (4) Each gun and team will take its own ammunition with it. 4000 per gun will be required.
Empty belts will be refilled immediately after returning to BATTLE positions.

WATER (5) O.C. No 2 Section will arrange for two tins of water to be at B5 position for the use of the section from 116 M.G.Co.

ZERO (6) ZERO will be notified later.

(7) ACKNOWLEDGE.

10/2/17

[signature]
Comm MGCoy.

Table of Gun Positions & Targets.

		Position	Targets
GROUP 1.	4 Guns 116 M.G. Co.	RAILWAY I 17 a 2.9½	IBEX SUPPORT IBERIA RESERVE
GROUP 2.	3 Guns (Lt RUTLEDGE)	ST. JAMES TR.	IBEX LANE IBEX SUPPORT
GROUP 3	3 Guns. (Lt BROOKE)	CONGREVE WALK	CAMEROON TRENCH " SUPPORT " AVENUE
GROUP 4	2 Guns (Lt SUTHERLAND)	GARDEN ST.	CAMEROON TRENCH " SUPPORT " RESERVE IBERIA AVENUE

SECRET Copy No 8

AMENDMENT to 117 M.G. Co. Order No 20.

PARA 2 is CANCELLED and the following substituted:-

OBJECTIVE (2) "A" raid will have as its objective:- front German line from I5 b 6.6.38 to C 29 d 4.0

"B" raid will have as its objective:- the enemy system of trenches from C 29 a 6.6 to C 29 a 45.67.

The raiding party will remain in the German trenches 25 minutes.

117 M.G. Co. ACTION (3) The Machine Gun Coy. Barrage will commence at ZERO minus 4.

MEDICAL (4) Casualties will be evacuated direct to R.A.P's at POTIJE CHATEAU for left Guns, and to AID POST at MENIN DUMP for RIGHT GUNS.

(5) O.C. No. 4 Section will arrange that the gun and team which is to be attached to 2nd Lt. SUTHERLAND is at ST JEAN at least 3 hours before ZERO.

O.C. No. 2 Section will arrange for the gun and team which is to be attached to 2nd Lt. RUTLEDGE to be at LEFT SECTION H.Q. in HAYMARKET at least 3 hours before ZERO, and also that the tripod with the team has an elevating and traversing dial.

(6) PROGRAMME for Z day.

ZERO minus 1 hour. All guns in position
10.0 P.M. Assembly of raiding party commences
10.50 P.M. Assembly in front line trenches complete.
ZERO minus 6. Assembly in No MAN'S LAND begins
ZERO minus 4. Machine Gun barrage commences
ZERO plus 25. First two BLUE ROCKETS go up and withdrawal commences.

<u>SECRET.</u>
<u>VERY IMPORTANT.</u>

13-2-17

At about ZERO plus 6 or ZERO plus 10 all our artillery fire will partially <u>cease fire</u> for a short time. <u>The machine gun barrage must also cease</u> at the same time and recommence when the artillery recommences. Great care therefore must be ~~taken~~ paid to our artillery.

A special N.C.O. or man will be posted at each gun to listen to our artillery and immediately he hears it dying down he will order his gun to cease fire.

This is very important and great care must be taken that the enemy retaliation is not mistaken for our own artillery fire.

H O Rees

ZERO plus 27 Second two BLUE
Rockets go up.

AMMUNITION (7) 10 Belt Boxes per gun
will be taken instead
of 16.

(8) ACKNOWLEDGE.

11/2/17

Copies to all recipients of
117 M.G. Co. Order No. 20.

[signature]
117 M.G. C.

SECRET. Copy No. 5....

117th INFANTRY BRIGADE ORDER No.127.

14.2.1917.

1. The 39th Division will be relieved by the 55th Division in the Right Divisional Sector commencing on the 15th February.

2. On relief of the 117th Infantry Brigade by the 165th Infantry Brigade (see Relief Table "A") the Brigade will be attached to the 38th Division as Divisional Reserve, and will be distributed in Camps and take over duties as shown in attached Location Table "B".

3. All details of relief not specified in these Orders will be arranged direct between Commanding Officers concerned.

4. Units will hand over on relief all work in hand and proposed, all Defence Schemes, Maps, Aeroplane Photographs, Trench Stores, etc., obtaining receipts.

5. The Relief of the Maintenance Parties in "P" Works will take place on February 15th. Relieving parties will report to Camp Adjutant, at "C" Camp at 11 a.m., 15th February. Returned parties will rejoin their Units on relief.

6. Administrative Orders for the relief and subsequent moves are being issued by the Staff Captain.

7. There will be no movement of Transport or Troops (except billetting and advance parties, etc.) EAST of VLAMERTINGHE before 5.15 p.m.daily.

8. Advance Parties will be sent on in each case on the morning of the day of relief to take over billets and area stores in the Camps and Billets occupied by the 166th Infantry Brigade.

9. Completion of all Reliefs will be at once reported in "BAB" Code to Brigade Headquarters.

10. Brigade Headquarters will close at RAMPARTS at 9.p.m. on the 17th., reopening at "D" Camp at the same hour.

11. ACKNOWLEDGE.

W.G. Maxwell Captain,

14.2.1917. Brigade Major, 117th Infantry Brigade.

Copies issued at 8 p.m.to:-

No.1. 16th Notts & Derby Regt.
2. 17th ditto
3. 17th K.R.R.Corps.
4. 16th Rifle Brigade.
5. 117th Machine Gun Coy.
6. 117th T.Mortar Battery.
7. H.Q's.,39th Division.
8. ditto
9. H.Q's.,165th Brigade.
10. " 164th "
11. " 113th "
12. " 114th "
13. " 118th "
14. " 116th "
No.15. H.Q's.,70th Brigade.
16. No.3 Coy.,Divl.Train.
17. Supply Officer,117th Bde.
18. 225th Field Coy.,R.E.
19. 177th Tunnelling Coy.
20. Right Group, R.A.
21. Town Major, Ypres.
22. Commandant, Ypres.
23. G.O.C.
24. B.M.
25. S.C.
26. B.S.O.
27&28. War Diary.
29. Order file.

TABLE "A".

RELIEF TABLE to accompany 117th INFANTRY BRIGADE ORDER No.127.

Item	Date.	Unit.	Relieved by.	From.	To.	Route.	Time & place for Platoon Guides for incoming Units.	Remarks.
1.	Feb.15th & Night 15/16th.	16th Notts & Derby Regt.	7th LIVERPOOL Regt.	Left Support Battalion.	"E" Camp.	Via YPRES - VLAMERTINGHE and BRANDHOEK.	ASYLUM Stn. Time will be notified later.	
2.		17th Ditto (less 1 Coy as in Item 3)	5th LIVERPOOL Regt.	Right Support Battalion.	"P" Camp.	ditto	ditto	This Battn will find PESELHOEK W. Party from 17th (inclusive).
3.		1 Coy.17th N.& D.(5 Officers,170 OR, & 3 Lewis Gs.	ditto	ditto	Front Line, LANCS. FARM Section.	DEAD END - BOESINGHE - YPRES Road.	C.25.c.3.8.(ESSEX Fm) 6 p.m. Guides from 14th R.W.F.	Comes under orders of 14th R.W.F., 113th Brigade.
4.	Feb.16th & Night 16/17th.	17th K.R.R. Corps.	5th LIVERPOOL Regt.	Right Front Battalion.	Right Support Battalion.	Any convenient.	As arranged between C.Os.	RELIEF is Not to commence before 5 p.m.
5.		16th Rifle Brigade.	7th LIVERPOOL Regt.	Left Front Battalion.	Left Support Battalion.	Any convenient.	ditto	ditto
6.		2 Coys.17th Notts & Derby Regt.	--	"P" Camp.	CANAL BANK.	Any convenient.	As arranged direct between 17th N.& D.Regt.& L/5 N.LANCS.Regt.	1 Coy.will be attached to each of the 113th & 114th Brigades.
7.	Feb.17th & Night 17/18th.	17th K.R.R. Corps.	6th LIVERPOOL Regt.	Right Support Battalion.	"D" Camp.	Via YPRES - VLAMERTINGHE and BRANDHOEK.	ASYLUM Stn. Time will be notified later.	
8.		16th Rifle Brigade.	9th LIVERPOOL Regt.	Left Support Battalion.	HOUTON Farm. B.14.a.2.8.	Via YPRES and VLAMERTINGHE.	ditto	Takes over Cable Burying Party of 200 diggers from 1/5 LANCS Regt from 18th.(incl.)

P.T.O.

TABLE "A" (continued).

Item.	Date.	Unit.	Relieved by.	From.	To.	Route.	Time and place for Platoon Guides for incoming Units.	Remarks.
9.	Feb.18th & Night 18/19th.	117th M.Gun Company.	165th M.Gun Company.	Line.	"S" Camp.	Via YPRES - VLAMERTINGHE - BRANDHOEK.	ASYLUM Stn. Time will be notified later.	
10.		117th Trench Mortar Bty.	165th Trench Mortar Bty.	Line.	"S" Camp.	ditto	ditto	
11.	Feb.20th.	117th M.Gun Company	--	"S" Camp.	BOESINGHE Section.	Any convenient.	As arranged direct between Os.C.,117th and 115th M.Gun Coys.	Relieves 115th Machine Gun Company.

TABLE "B".

LOCATION AND WORK TABLE.

Unit.	Location on completion of relief.	DAILY WORKING PARTIES.		
		Strength	Locality and Nature.	Date when work starts.
16th Notts & Derby Regt.	"E" Camp.	50 men. 10 men.	Camp "J" Camp "H"	17.2.17. 17.2.17.
17th Notts & Derby Regt.	(a) Battn.H.Q's and 1 Coy:- "P" Camp. (b) 1 Coy.(to include 5 Officers, 170 Other Ranks, 3 Lewis Guns) attached 14th R.W.F. (LANCS.Farm Section). (c) 2 Coys. attached respectively to 113th and 114th Brigades, 38th Div.	3 N.C.Os 25 men.	PESELHOEK R.E.Yard.	17.2.17.
17th K.R.R. Corps.	"D" Camp.	30 men. 2 N.C.Os & 20 men.	Cable Burying near Camp "D". Collecting Rubble.	18.2.17. 18.2.17.
16th Rifle Brigade.	MOUTON FARM. B.14.a.2.8.	280 men. 2 N.C.Os 20 men.	Cable Burying. Screening Parties.	18.2.17. 18.2.17.
117th Machine Gun Company.	BOESINGHE Section.	--	--	--
117th Trench Mortar Bty.	"S" Camp.	--	--	--
117th Brigade Headquarters.	"D" Camp.	--	--	--

SECRET.

Copy No. 5....

117th INFANTRY BRIGADE ORDER No. 124.

9.2.1917.

Reference: St. JULIEN Sheet 28 N.W. 1/10,000.
NO MAN'S LAND Map, 1/2000.

The day of operations is referred to throughout as "Z" Day.

INTENTION. 1. The G.O.C., 39th Division, intends to carry out the following Raids, with a view to inflicting losses on the enemy, securing prisoners and indentifications, and damaging his trenches as much as possible.

OBJECTIVE. 2. "A" Raid will have as its objective:-

Front German Line from I.5.b.66.30. to C.29.d.4.0.
German Support Line I.5.b.75.45. to I.5.b.58.90.

"B" Raid will have as its objective:-

C.29.a.53.60., C.23.c.25.00. and German Support Line C.29.a.75.80 to C.23.c.53.07.

3. (a) The 16th RIFLE BRIGADE will carry out "A" Raid. The 1/1st HERTS Regt. will carry out "B" Raid.

(b) The strength of the Raiding Party of the 16th RIFLE BRIGADE will be 330 All Ranks.

4. The Raid will be carried out as follows:-

Preliminary Assembly will take place in our front trenches - HAYMARKET on the Right (inclusive) to POTIJZE Road (inclusive).

The advance will be carried out in four waves; the two leading waves after crossing the Front Line German Trench will go straight to the German Support Line; the third and fourth waves will occupy the German Front Line.

FLANK PROTECTION. 5. (i) O.C., 16th NOTTS & DERBY Regiment, will detail one Platoon and Lewis Gun to act as Right Flanking party. They will take up their position in the neighbourhood of I.5.b.5.$\frac{1}{2}$., pushing out strong Standing Patrols into the Saps running from the German Front Line to I.5.b.6.1. near the MOAT and the German Listening Post at I.5.b.4$\frac{1}{2}$.2$\frac{1}{2}$. These patrols will push well up these Saps, and prevent any hostile parties trying to outflank the Raid. The main body of the Flanking Party must be placed so as to keep in touch with these patrols.

Position of Assembly:- Trench I.5.6.

(ii) O.C., 16th RIFLE BRIGADE, will detail one Platoon to act as Left Flanking Party. They will establish themselves in the old trenches just North of the POTIJZE Road, and push out a strong Patrol in ODER HO.

Position of Assembly:- Trench C.29.1.

Both these Flanking Parties will be in their Assembly positions at Zero minus one hour. They will advance into NO MAN'S LAND at Zero minus 2.
Most careful reconnaissance by Officers and N.C.Os will be made on "W", "X" and "Y" Nights.

P.T.O. 6./

6. The G.O.C., 118th Infantry Brigade, will be asked to maintain half his usual garrison in our Assembly Trenches, and not less than four Lewis Guns. During the Assembly this garrison will withdraw to its dug-outs, but immediately take up their positions after the fourth wave has gone over.

ARTILLERY ACTION. 7. The Right Group, 39th Divisional Artillery, and the Corps Heavy Artillery, will support the attack. The action of the Field Artillery is given in the sub-joined table "A"

MACHINE GUN ACTION. 8. The 117th Machine Gun Company (eight guns), and one section, 116th Machine Gun Company, will cover the flanks of the Raid with intense fire. Their targets will be as laid down in the sub-joined table "B" Guns will be in position at Zero minus one hour.

LIGHT TRENCH MORTAR ACTION. 9. The 117th Trench Mortar Battery will bring four Stokes Mortars into action on each flank of the Raid. Their targets will be as laid down in sub-joined table "C."

R.E. AND DEMOLITIONS. 10. (a) O.C., 225th Coy., R.E., will place at the disposal of O.C., 16th Rifle Brigade, one N.C.O. and ten sappers for Demolition purposes. They should be provided with Demolition charges for machine gun emplacements and dugouts, which will be placed in position, but not ignited until the withdrawal from any given line is just on the point of being completed.

O.C., Company, will please arrange with O.C., 16th Rifle Brigade, for rehearsal of his men with the attacking troops, and a demonstration of Demolition.

(b) A proportion of the "Moppers-up" will carry P.Bombs which will be ignited just as the withdrawal from any given line is being completed. They will be placed in dugouts and the trenches, with a view to destroying woodwork and revetments. There will be one P.Bomb for every 30 yards of front.

PRISONERS. 11. All Prisoners will be sent direct to Brigade Headquarters. Papers and trophies will be brought to Brigade Headquarters by the Raid Intelligence Officer as soon as possible after the completion of the raid. One Officer will be detailed by O.C., 16th Rifle Brigade, as special Searching and Intelligence Officer.

COMMUNICATIONS. 12. (i) From German Front Line (Command Post) by runner to our front line, thence by Relay Post to NEW COTTS, thence to MILL COTTS (Advanced Battn. Headquarters), thence to Advanced Brigade Headquarters.

(ii) By telephone from Advanced Battalion to Brigade Headquarters.

MEDICAL. 13. Casualties will be evacuated direct to the 2 R.A.P's at POTIJZE CHATEAU ~~and Right Battalion Headquarters~~. There will be:-

(i) An Advanced R.Aid Post in the position of Assembly for first aid, but there is no dug-out and it will have to be in the open trench about I.5.a.9½.8½.

(ii) Advanced Aid Post at I.5.b.1.4. in the front line trench.

Contd. Routes/

Routes of evacuation.

(i) The POTIJZE Road by wheeled and hand stretchers via NEW COTTS and MILL COTTS (Relay Post) direct to CHATEAU.

(ii) HAYMARKET, Communication Trench for Walking Cases only.

(iii) A flagged route over the open (if the frost holds) as far as CAMBRIDGE Trench (Relay Post) thence to MILL COTTS, thence to CHATEAU A.D.S.

Post.	Personnel.
Adv.Aid Post, I.5.b.1.4.	8 Regtl. Stretcher Bearers.
Relay Post, CAMBRIDGE Tr.) I.5.a.4.5.)	8 ditto
Adv.Aid Post, I.5.a.9½.8.	8 ditto
MILL COTTS. Relay Post.	16 R. A. M. C.

PREPARA-TIONS. 14. The following preparations on "Y" and "Z" nights will be carried out as under:-

"Y" Night. O.C., 16th Rifle Brigade, will arrange to place his "Gap" Boards in position, and cut lanes through our wire to within 12'0" of the outer edge.
The Brigade Intelligence Officer will flag out a stretcher route from CAMBRIDGE Trench North of HAYMARKET to MILL COTTS.

"Z" Day. O.C., 16th Notts & Derby Regiment, will detail a party to build up the duckboard ramps with materials already in position, at each passing-out place.

The O.C., 16th Notts & Derby Regiment, will be responsible for placing a thick layer of earth on the duckboards in HAYMARKET during "Z" Day. Materials should be gathered ready for this, and men stationed at intervals to re-spread earth just previous to the time of the Raid.

"Z" Night. As soon as it is dark the remainder of the wire will be cleared, and taping out operations will take place by parties of the 16th Rifle Brigade.

O.C., 16th Rifle Brigade, will instal a Rocket Station (to be drawn from Brigade Headquarters) in CAMBRIDGE Trench.

[A]DVANCED [HE]AD-[QU]ARTERS. 15. 16th RIFLE BRIGADE: At MILL COTTS.

117th Infantry BRIGADE: At LEFT Battalion Headquarters.

[Z]ERO. 16. ZERO will be notified later, and instructions for synchronisation of watches issued in due course.

17. ACKNOWLEDGE.

A.S. Fetherstonhaugh Captain,

[.].2.1917. for Brigade Major, 117th Infantry Brigade.

(P.T.O. for distribution of copies).

Copies issued to:-

No.1. 16th Notts & Derby Regt.
2. 17th ditto
3. 17th K.R.R.Corps.
4. 16th Rifle Brigade.
5. 117th Machine Gun Coy.
6. 117th Trench Mortar Bty.
7. H.Q's.,39th Division.
8. ditto
9. H.Q's.,116th Brigade.
10. H.Q's.,118th Brigade.
11. H.Q's.,70th Brigade.
12. C.R.A.,39th Division.

No.13. C.R.E.,39th Division.
14. A.D.M.S., ditto
15. O.C.,225 Coy.,R.E.
16. O.C.Right Group, R.A.
17. G.O.C.
18. B.M.
19. S.C.
20. B.I.O.
21. B.S.O.
22. B.B.O.
23. O.C.,177th Tunnelling Coy.
24. Order File.

25 and 26 War Diary.

TABLE "A".

RAID BARRAGE (18 pounders).

Unit.	Time.	Guns.	Task.	Ammunition.	Rate.
RIGHT Group.	Zero minus 4'.	18.	Open on line 50 yards short of German Front Line C.29.d.30.10 to I.5.b.65.37. and remain there till Zero minus 2'.	Shrapnel.	4 rounds per gun per minute.
	Zero minus 2'.		Lift 50 yards.		
	Zero minus 1'.		Lift 50 yards.		
	Zero		Lift and reach German Support Line and remain on that for one minute.		
	Zero plus 1'.		Lift 100 yards.		
	Zero plus 2'.		Lift 100 yards.		
	Zero plus 3'.		Lift and reach IBERIA Reserve Line.		
	Zero plus 4'.		Form BOX BARRAGE.		
A277.		6	I.5.b.65.37 to I.5.b.45.57.		
A174.		6	I.5.b.45.87 to I.5.b.42.84.		
B174.		6	I.5.b.42.84 to C.29.d.30.10.		
			BOX BARRAGE.		
A277.	Zero plus 4' to plus 47'	(2 (4	IBEX Avenue I.6.a.4.4. IBERIA Reserve I.6.a.3.4 to I.6.a.13.65.		
A174.		6	IBERIA Reserve I.6.a.13.65 to Outpost Buildings C.29.d.96.12.	H.E.	1½ rounds per gun per minute.
B174.		(2 (4	CAMEROON Avenue C.30.c.00.42. C.29.d.45.60. to C.29.1.46.37.		

Continued - P.T.O.

TABLE "A" (continued).

RAID BARRAGE (4.5" Howitzers).

Unit.	Time.	Guns.	Task.	Ammunition.	Rate.
ASSAULT BARRAGE.					
D174.	Zero minus 4 to Zero plus 4.	3 1	OSKAR FAR. Salient. Trench Junction I.6.a.3.4.	H.E.	2 rounds per gun per minute.
D275.	ditto	1 3.	Trench Junction I.6.a.4.4. Outpost buildings.		
C179.	ditto	4	IBERIA Reserve.		
BOX BARRAGE.					
C179.	Zero plus 4' to plus 47'.	2 2	CAMEROON Reserve. C.29.d.95.25 to 85.45. IBEX LANE.	"	1 round per gun per minute.
D174.	ditto	4.	As for Assault Barrage.		
D275.	ditto	4.	As for Assault Barrage.		

T A B L E "B".

ACTION OF M A C H I N E G U N S.

Group I.	Four Guns (116th M.G. Company).	-	RAILWAY I.17.a.2.9½.
		Targets:	IBEX Support, IBERIA Reserve.
Group II.	Three Guns	-	ST. JAMES Trench.
		Targets:	IBEX Lane. IBEX Support.
Group III.	Three Guns	-	CONGREVE WALK.
		Targets:	CAMEROON Trench, Support and AVENUE.
Group IV.	Two Guns	-	GARDEN Street.
		Targets:	CAMEROON Trench, SUPPORT and RESERVE, and IBERIA Avenue.

T A B L E "C".

ACTION of L I G H T T R E N C H M O R T A R S.

DISPOSITIONS:

2 Mortars - C.29.1., C.29.2.
2 Mortars - C.29.3½.
2 Mortars - I.5.4.
2 Mortars - I.5.2.

Mortar.	Objectives.	Rate of fire.
No.1.	I.6.c.0.9. to I.6.c.2.7½.	
No.2.	I.6.c.2.9½.to I.6.c.3.7.	Four rounds
No.3.	I.6.a.½.2½.to I.6.c.2.9.	per gun per
No.4.	I.5.b.9.2. to I.5.d.9¾.8.	minute =
No.5.	C.29.d.7.2.to C.29.d.6.4½.	2080 or 260
No.6.	C.29.d.6.4½.to C.29.d.4.7.	rounds per
No.7.	C.29.d.4.1. to C.29.d.4.3½.	gun.
No.8.	C.29.d.4.3½. to C.29.d.4.7.	

SECRET.

Copy No.....5

AMENDMENT to 117th INFANTRY BRIGADE ORDER No. 124.

11.2.1917.

Paras 2, 3 and 4 are CANCELLED and the following SUBSTITUTED:-

OBJECTIVE. 2. "A" Raid will have as its objective:-

Front German Line from I.5.b.66.38 to C.29.d.4.0.

"B" Raid will have as its objective:-

The enemy system of trenches from C.29.a.6.6. to C.29.a.45.67.

3. (a) The 16th RIFLE BRIGADE will carry out "A" Raid. The 1/1st HERTS Regt. will carry out "B" Raid.

(b) The strength of the Raiding Party of the 16th RIFLE BRIGADE will be approximately 120 All Ranks including 4 Officers.

4. The Raid will be carried out as follows:-

Preliminary Assembly will take place in our front trenches - HAYMARKET on the Right (inclusive) to POTIJZE Road on the Left (inclusive).
The Assembly in No Man's Land will take place as quietly as possible along the taped out assembly lines.

The attack will be carried out in two waves in three groups -

RIGHT Group directed on the Gap in German Wire about I.5.b.50.45.
This party will comprise the detachment for EITELFRITZ Farm.

CENTRE Group will enter by the Gap at the point of the MOUND.

LEFT Group will move direct on the Gap at I.5.b.45.82.

The party directed on the MOUND will immediately make good the sap leading to the front German Trench, and establish connection towards the Left and Right parties.

The Right Party will move to its left, and get in touch with the MOUND Party. In order to prevent bombing each other, this should be carried out "over the top".

Similarly the Left Party will establish connection with its Right.

The results of Drill Barrages have clearly shown that the enemy is ready to put down his counter-barrage on our front trenches. It is therefore essential that the Assembly in No Man's Land should take place as quietly as possible, and the whole Raiding Force be well clear of our trenches before our barrage begins.

The Raiding Party will remain in the German Trenches 25 minutes.

Flank /

FLANK PROTECTION.	Para 5 (ii).	This Platoon of the 16th RIFLE BRIGADE will include one Lewis Gun.
		The Right and Left Flanking Parties will withdraw to our trenches 15 minutes after the withdrawal of the Raiding Party is complete, i.e. at Zero plus 60.
MACHINE GUN ACTION.	Para.8.	The Machine Gun Company Barrage will commence at Zero minus 4.
LIGHT TRENCH MORTAR ACTION.	Para.9.	The Trench Mortar Bombardment will commence at Zero minus 4.
R.E. AND DEMOLITIONS.	Para.10.	The R.E. Party will be reduced to 1 N.C.O. and 6 men.
PRISONERS.	Para.11.	No prisoner will be interrogated by anyone on the road to Brigade Headquarters.
		Specimens of Rations are to be made particular care of by the Searching and Intelligence Officer.
MEDICAL.	Para.13 (iii).	Evacuation by the Flagged Route over the open is cancelled, but the Relay Post in CAMBRIDGE Trench will still be posted by the 16th Rifle Brigade.
		The Relay Post at MILL COTTS of 16 R.A.M.C. Bearers is allotted the Northern Entrance to the Dugouts there, as their Station.

ACKNOWLEDGE.

A. A. Fetherstonhaugh Captain,

11.2.1917.

for Brigade Major, 117th Infantry Brigade.

Copies issued to all Recipients of 117th Infantry Brigade Order No.124.

T A B L E "D".

P R O G R A M M E for "Z" DAY.

6 p.m.	Tapes for Assembly in NO MAN'S LAND put out
7 p.m.	Concertinas removed from Gaps in our wire.
8.45 p.m.	Drill Barrage on RAID OBJECTIVE.
9.30 p.m.	Hot Tea and Rum served out at Left Battalion H.Q's.
10 p.m.	Assembly by HAYMARKET and POTIJZE Road commences.
10.50 p.m.	Assembly in Front Line Trenches complete.
Zero minus 6.	Assembly in NO MAN'S LAND begins.
Zero minus 4.	Field Artillery opens Barrage on line 50 yards short of German Front Line. Machine Gun and Light Trench Mortar Barrages commence.
Zero minus 2 to Zero plus 25.	Artillery action according to TABLE "A".
Zero plus 25.	First two BLUE ROCKETS go up and Withdrawal commences.) From CAMBRIDGE Trench.
Zero plus 27.	Second two BLUE ROCKETS go up.) From CAMBRIDGE Trench.

SECRET. Copy No. 5

SECOND AMENDMENT
to
117th INFANTRY BRIGADE ORDER No.124.

12.2.1917.

Para 5 (ii) of FIRST AMENDMENT will read as follows:-

"This Platoon of 16th RIFLE BRIGADE will include
"one Lewis Gun.

"The Right and Left Flanking Parties will withdraw
"to our trenches 15 minutes after the withdrawal
"of the Raiding Party is complete, i.e. at Zero
"plus 40."

M. Fetherstonhaugh Captain,

12.2.1917. for Brigade Major, 117th Infantry Brigade.

Copies issued to all recipients of 117th Infantry Brigade
Order No.124.

Instructions regarding War Diaries and Intelligence Summaries are contained in F. S. Regs., Part II. and the Staff Manual respectively. Title pages will be prepared in manuscript.

WAR DIARY
or
~~INTELLIGENCE SUMMARY.~~
(Erase heading not required.)

Army Form C. 2118.

117 M.G. Co.
Vol XI

Place	Date	Hour	Summary of Events and Information	Remarks and references to Appendices
YPRES	1/3/17		Enemy artillery active during day & MGs at night. ~~Ypres~~ YPRES shelled during the day. Bombardment on our right at 10 pm. Work done on mined dugouts & emplacements under supervision of R.E. 250 Rounds fired on Barrage line by gun in ROSSLYN ST.	
"	2/3/17		Enemy artillery active during day. Ypres shelled very heavily during afternoon especially near LILLE GATE. Coy mess blown in by direct hit. Cook killed & 2 servants wounded. Work done on mined dugouts & emplacements under RE supervision.	
"	3/3/17		Artillery active YPRES shelled during the day. Enemy's MGs active at night. Our artillery very active at 11 pm. Work done on M.G. emplacements & dugouts under RE's.	
"	4/3/17		Artillery active during day & MGs at night. Work done under R.E.s	

2353 Wt. W2544/1454 700,000 5/15 D. D. & L. A.D.S.S./Forms/C. 2118.

Instructions regarding War Diaries and Intelligence Summaries are contained in F. S. Regs., Part II. and the Staff Manual respectively. Title pages will be prepared in manuscript.

Army Form C. 2118.

WAR DIARY
or
~~INTELLIGENCE SUMMARY.~~
(Erase heading not required.)

Place	Date	Hour	Summary of Events and Information	Remarks and references to Appendices
Sector [illegible]	5/3/17.		Enemy artillery active during day & night. MGs active at night — Work done on MG emplacements & dugouts under RE supervision. Dugouts & emplacements cleaned and repaired. 2000 Rounds fired at STIRLING CASTLE & trenches in neighborhood.	
"	6/3/17		Artillery activity on both sides during day & night. MGs active at night. Work done on pumping & construction concrete [illegible] & tunnels, MG emplacements & dugouts under RE supervision. Ammunition cleaned & Belts refilled. Dugouts & emplacements cleaned and repaired. 2000 Rounds fired at STIRLING CASTLE & trenches in neighborhood.	
"	7/3/17		Enemy Artillery active. MG's active at night. Work done under RE supervision on Concrete & mined Dugouts & emplacements.	
	8/3/17		Fairly quiet day & night. Intermittent artillery activity. MGs active at night. Work done under RE.	
~				

2353 Wt. W2544/1454 700,000 5/15 D. D. & L. A.D.S.S./Forms/C. 2118.

Instructions regarding War Diaries and Intelligence Summaries are contained in F. S. Regs., Part II. and the Staff Manual respectively. Title pages will be prepared in manuscript.

WAR DIARY
or
~~INTELLIGENCE SUMMARY.~~
(Erase heading not required.)

Army Form C. 2118.

Place	Date	Hour	Summary of Events and Information	Remarks and references to Appendices
Ypres	9/3/17		Enemy artillery active at intervals, M.G's active at night. Otherwise very quiet. The Coy was relieved by the 118 M.G.Co & after relief proceeded to ERIE CAMP.	
ERIE CAMP	10/3/17		Rest & training	
" "	11/3/17		Training.	
" "	12/3/17		do	
" "	13/3/17		do	
" "	14/3/17		The Coy was inspected by GEN PLUMER commanding 2nd ARMY.	
" "	15/3/17		The Coy relieved the 118 M.G.Co in the Left Brigade Sector. Coy H.Q. at YPRES.	
YPRES	16/3/17		Enemy M.G's active during night. YPRES shelled about 8pm, otherwise quiet	
"	17/3/17		Enemy artillery active at intervals during day & night ~~[illegible]~~ & M.G's at night, otherwise quiet. Work done on pumping & building Concrete M.G. Emplacements & dugouts under R.E.s. Ammunition cleaned & belts refilled.	
"	18/3/17		Considerable activity during the day both on the front line and in Ypres. M.G's active at night on the MENIN Road and	

Instructions regarding War Diaries and Intelligence Summaries are contained in F. S. Regs., Part II. and the Staff Manual respectively. Title pages will be prepared in manuscript.

WAR DIARY

or

~~INTELLIGENCE SUMMARY.~~

(Erase heading not required.)

Army Form C. 2118.

Place	Date	Hour	Summary of Events and Information	Remarks and references to Appendices
YPRES	18/3/17		and CULVERT Locality. Enemy aircraft very active. One seen to come down apparently in difficulties, behind his lines on the left. Three enemy engaged 2 British at 12.10pm. One British brought down. Work done under RE supervision on Concrete trunked dugouts & emplacements.	
"	19/3/17		Marked decrease in Artillery. 77mm fired on Support & Reserve Trenches. Bund was fired on at 3pm. Increase in activity of TMs. Five were active both in daylight & night. Work done on TMs emplacements & dugouts under RE supervision	
"	20/3/17		An exceptionally quiet day. A few rounds were fired on I.22.b.8.5. No TMs activity. Ours 500 Rounds fired on Chateaux Wood. 500 " on trench at I.13.a.8.3. 1000 " on Tramway in front of STIRLING CASTLE.	

2353 Wt. W2544/1454 700,000 5/15 D. D. & L. A.D.S.S./Forms/C. 2118.

Army Form C. 2118.

WAR DIARY
or
~~INTELLIGENCE SUMMARY.~~
(Erase heading not required.)

Instructions regarding War Diaries and Intelligence Summaries are contained in F. S. Regs., Part II. and the Staff Manual respectively. Title pages will be prepared in manuscript.

Place	Date	Hour	Summary of Events and Information	Remarks and references to Appendices
YPRES.	20/3/17		Work done on concrete & mined dugouts under RE supervision. Pumping out deep dugouts at RITZ ST & MAPLE ST. Empl & dugouts cleaned & repaired.	
"	21/3/17		Increase in ~~enemy~~ artillery activity. Ypres shelled frequently during the day & also ZILLEBEKE BUND. BROKEN Bridge was also shelled during the morning. Work done on Concrete MG Em & dugouts under RE supervision. Emplacements & dugouts cleaned and repaired.	
"	22/3/17		YPRES constantly shelled. 1000 rounds fired at JACKDAW & trenches during night. 1000 — — — CHATEAUX WOOD " " 500 — — — J 13 d 7 3 " "	
"	23/3/17		YPRES constantly shelled especially round LILLE GATE. 1000 rounds fired at tramway from JACKDAW to STIRLING CASTE. 1000 — — — — — — J 19 b 5 5	

2353 Wt. W2544/1454 700,000 5/15 D. D. & L. A.D.S.S./Forms/C. 2118.

Instructions regarding War Diaries and Intelligence Summaries are contained in F. S. Regs., Part II. and the Staff Manual respectively. Title pages will be prepared in manuscript.

WAR DIARY
or
~~INTELLIGENCE SUMMARY.~~
(Erase heading not required.)

Army Form C. 2118.

Place	Date	Hour	Summary of Events and Information	Remarks and references to Appendices
YPRES	24/3/17		YPRES constantly shelled also ZILLEBEEKE BUND. Company headquarters hit 3 casualties (one of whom Pte Moore died of wounds).	
			500 rounds fired at STIRLING CASTLE during the night	
"	25/3/17		YPRES considerably shelled during afternoon & evening	
			1000 rounds fired at STIRLING CASTLE during night	
			1000 " " road " J19b	
			200 - - - enemy aeroplane about 9 am	
			6250 - - - on S.O.S. lines about 12.30 a.m. 26/3/17 when enemy raided adjoining sector on the right and barraged our front line on the right.	
	26/3/17		Enemy artillery very much quieter.	
			1000 fired at CHATEAU WOOD and STIRLING CASTLE during night	
			1000 - - STIRLING CASTLE and strong point in vicinity.	
			Usual work continued nightly under RE in constructing tunnelled emplacements and dug outs in WELLINGTON CRESCENT ~~...~~ RITZ ST, + GORDON HO.	

Army Form C. 2118.

Instructions regarding War Diaries and Intelligence Summaries are contained in F. S. Regs., Part II. and the Staff Manual respectively. Title pages will be prepared in manuscript.

WAR DIARY

or

~~INTELLIGENCE SUMMARY.~~

(Erase heading not required.)

Place	Date	Hour	Summary of Events and Information.	Remarks and references to Appendices
ERIE CAMP	27.3.17		Training in Rest billets	
"	28.3.17		" " "	
"	29.3.17		" " "	
"	30.3.17		" " "	
"	31.3.17		" " "	

for Dalleal Lt.

O.C. No. 117th Coy. Machine Gun Corps.

2353 Wt. W2544/1454 700,000 5/15 D. D. & L. A.D.S.S./Forms/C. 2118.

Army Form C. 2118.

Instructions regarding War Diaries and Intelligence Summaries are contained in F. S. Regs., Part II. and the Staff Manual respectively. Title pages will be prepared in manuscript.

WAR DIARY
or
~~INTELLIGENCE SUMMARY.~~
(Erase heading not required.)

117 M G Coy
Vol 12

Place	Date	Hour	Summary of Events and Information	Remarks and references to Appendices
ERIE CAMP	1.4.17		Training in Rest Billets. 2 O.R. to base JHR	
YPRES	2.4.17		The Coy relieved the 118 M.G. Coy in the left Brigade Sector. Coy Hqurs at YPRES JHR	
"	3.4.17		YPRES shelled during the afternoon and evening. Enemy M.Guns active during the	
"			night. The ZILLEBEKE BUND shelled at 1 p.m. JHR	
"	4.4.17		ZILLEBEKE BUND shelled at 1 P.M. Enemy sent up a green rocket dividing into several stars, opposite WELLINGTON CRESENT JHR	
	5.4.17		Enemy artillery quiet. - ours short bombardment at "Stand-to" - an enemy two starred green rocket observed North of MENIN ROAD JHR	
	6.4.17		Enemy artillery very active at intervals - big enemy strafe of YPRES about 5 p.m. One red floating light observed on our right followed by two green floating lights at 9 p.m. 4 O.R. Reinforcements JHR	
	7.4.17		Our guns bombarded on our left starting at 5.10 a.m. - Enemy sent up green and red rockets during the bombardment JHR	
	8.4.17		Heavy bombardment on our right by both sides beginning at 7.50 p.m. and ending at 9.15 p.m. - Enemy use GOLDEN RAIN SPRAY ROCKETS - his artillery opened immediately afterwards. Lt Rees + 2Lt A S Lawrence to England sick JHR	

2353 Wt. W2541/1454 700,000 5/15 D. D. & L. A.D.S.S./Forms/C 2118.

Instructions regarding War Diaries and Intelligence Summaries are contained in F. S. Regs., Part II. and the Staff Manual respectively. Title pages will be prepared in manuscript.

WAR DIARY
or
INTELLIGENCE SUMMARY.

(Erase heading not required.)

Army Form C. 2118.

Place	Date	Hour	Summary of Events and Information	Remarks and references to Appendices
YPRES.	9.4.17		The enemy continued throughout the day with the usual spasmodic shelling. Enemy observation balloon brought down behind Hooge by our airmen. Lt D.P. PLAYFAIR joined Coy. 1 OR to CCS 17 O.R. reinforcements JHR	
"	10.4.17		Relieved in the line by the 116 Coy. M.G.C. Coy then proceeded to ERIE CAMP	
ERIE CAMP	11.4.17		Training in Rest Billets JHR	
" "	12.4.17		" " " " JHR	
" "	13.4.17		Moved to MERCKEGHEM to rest. JHR	
MERCKEGHEM	14.4.17		Coy training in Rest Billets JHR	
"	15.4.17		" " " " " JHR	
"	16.4.17		" " " " JHR	
"	17.4.17		" " " " " JHR 45 attd men returned to their Battns	RoR
"	18.4.17		" " " " " 5 O.R. Reinforcements JHR	
"	19.4.17		" " " " " JHR	
"	20.4.17		" " " " " 1 OR to CCS JHR	
"	21.4.17		" " " " " JHR	
"	22.4.17		" " " " " JHR	

2353 Wt. W2541/1454 700,000 5/15 D. D. & L. A.D.S.S./Forms/C. 2118.

Instructions regarding War Diaries and Intelligence Summaries are contained in F. S. Regs., Part II. and the Staff Manual respectively. Title pages will be prepared in manuscript.

WAR DIARY
or
~~INTELLIGENCE SUMMARY.~~

(Erase heading not required.)

Army Form C. 2118.

Place	Date	Hour	Summary of Events and Information	Remarks and references to Appendices
MERCKEGHEM	23.4.17		Coy training in Rest Billets JHR	
"	24.4.17		" " " " " JHR	
"	25.4.17		" " " " " JHR	
"	26.4.17		" " " " " 19 OR transferred to 118 Coy M.G.C. JHR	
"	27.4.17		Coy moved to "Z" Camp. JHR	
"Z" Camp.	28.4.17		Coy training in Rest Billets JHR Capt Dunn Reported for instruction JHR	
"	29.4.17		" " " " " JHR	
"	30.4.17		Coy moved to "S" Camp. JHR	
~~"S" Camp~~	~~1.4.17~~		~~Coy training in rest billets.~~	

J. H. Rutledge Lt.
for O.C. No. 117th Coy.
Machine Gun Corps.

[illegible] Major
O.C. No. 117th Coy.
Machine Gun Corps.

2353 Wt. W2544/1454 700,000 5/15 D. D. & L. A.D.S.S./Forms/C. 2118.

Army Form C. 2118. 39

WAR DIARY
or
~~INTELLIGENCE SUMMARY~~

(Erase heading not required.)

117 . M.G. Company

Vol 13

Instructions regarding War Diaries and Intelligence Summaries are contained in F. S. Regs., Part II. and the Staff Manual respectively. Title Pages will be prepared in manuscript.

Place	Date	Hour	Summary of Events and Information	Remarks and references to Appendices
"5" Camp	1.5.17		Training in Rest Billets J.H.R.	
"	2.5.17		" " " " J.H.R.	
"	3.5.17		" " " " 3 men transferred to 113 Coy, 2 men " " 176 " 1 man " " 164 " 4 men " " 165 " } J.H.R.	
"	4.5.17		" " " " J.H.R.	
"	5.5.17		" " " " J.H.R.	
"	6.5.17		" " " " J.H.R.	
"	7.5.17		" " " " J.H.R.	
"	8.5.17		" " " " J.H.R.	
"	9.5.17		" " " " 1 off reinforcement "Lt A.C. MONTAGUE. J.H.R.	
"	10.5.17		" " " " J.H.R	
"	11.5.17		" " " " 1 O.R. transferred to 119 Coy M.G.C. J.H.R	
"	12.5.17		" " " " J.H.R	
"				

2449 Wt. W14957/M90 750,000 1/16 J.B.C. & A. Forms/C.2118/12.

Instructions regarding War Diaries and Intelligence Summaries are contained in F. S. Regs., Part II. and the Staff Manual respectively. Title Pages will be prepared in manuscript.

WAR DIARY
or
~~INTELLIGENCE SUMMARY~~

(Erase heading not required.)

117 MG Company

Army Form C. 2118.

Place	Date	Hour	Summary of Events and Information	Remarks and references to Appendices
"S" CAMP.	13.5.17		Training in Rest Billets JHR 1 O.R. attd as artificer JHR	
"	14.5.17		" " " 1. O.R. to C.C.S. JHR.	
"	15.5.17		" " " Lt NEALE. H.A. struck off strength Auth. A.C. 461 dated 15.5.17 J.H.R.	
	16.5.17		" " " JHR	
HILL TOP SECTOR	16.5.17		Relieved the 115 Machine Gun Company in the line JHR.	
"	17.5.17.		Heavy bombardment heard SOUTH of WILSON FARM. Enemy S.O.S seen from the same position in the direction of bombardment. A few enemy shells dropped about 1500 yds in front of LA BRIQUE position. Enemy machine guns and snipers active during the night J.H.R.	
"	18.5.17		Artillery activity on night at 8.45 pm to 9.30 p.m. Red rockets were observed bursting into two red stars at intervals during the bombardment. J.H.R	
"	19.5.17		Our S.O.S went up at 9.30 p.m. All the guns firing on S.O.S lines fired, expending a total of 13000 (thirteen thousand) rounds. Enemy S.O.S observed immediately our artillery barrage opened. JHR 1. O.R. to C.C.S. J.H.R.	

2449 Wt. W14957/M90 750,000 1/16 J.B.C. & A. Forms/C.2118/12.

Instructions regarding War Diaries and Intelligence Summaries are contained in F. S. Regs., Part II. and the Staff Manual respectively. Title Pages will be prepared in manuscript.

WAR DIARY
or
~~INTELLIGENCE SUMMARY~~

(Erase heading not required.)

117 M.G Company

Army Form C. 2118.

Place	Date	Hour	Summary of Events and Information	Remarks and references to Appendices
HILL TOP SECTOR	20.5.17		Hostile artillery bombardment at 9.30 p.m. Heavies were dropped in the vicinity of C26.2 position. Hostile machine Gun fired at intervals during the night over HILL TOP.	
			2Lt F. H. BELL. Reinforcement. J.H.R	
"	21.5.17		A small calibre shell burst close to emplacement at IRISH FARM. No damage done to emplacement. Remainder of period calm. J.H.R.	
"	22.5.17		Heavy bombardment by our artillery on our right commencing at 9.45 p.m. Enemy observed to put up the following lights (a) Gold + Silver Rain (b) Green Very lights.	
"	23.5.17		Heavy bombardment apparently on extreme right of Salient. Five enemy aeroplanes were observed over HILL TOP between 5 and 7 P.M. 22.5.17. Casualty 1 O.R. killed. J.H.R.	
"	24.5.17		Enemy trenches raided on right of salient after a heavy bombardment during afternoon + evening. Enemy M. Gun firing over HILL TOP located C15d 68.45 J.H.R	

2449 Wt. W14957/M90 750,000 1/16 J.B.C. & A. Forms/C.2118/12.

Instructions regarding War Diaries and Intelligence Summaries are contained in F. S. Regs., Part II. and the Staff Manual respectively. Title Pages will be prepared in manuscript.

WAR DIARY
or
~~INTELLIGENCE SUMMARY~~
(Erase heading not required.)

117 MG Company.

Army Form C. 2118.

Place	Date	Hour	Summary of Events and Information	Remarks and references to Appendices
HILL TOP SECTOR	25.5.17		Bombardment on right of Salient between 11 + 12 p.m. BILGE TRENCH shelled by enemy with 4.2 howitzers. Enemy machine guns and snipers very active during the night in the vicinity of THE WILLOWS. JHR.	
"	26.5.17		ST JEAN was heavily shelled by the enemy from 6.15 p.m to 7.15 p.m. Two enemy aeroplanes flew over our lines between 5 and 6 a.m this morning. JHR.	
"	27.5.17		Our Artillery very active. Hostile machine guns active at "Stand to". Enemy aeroplane seen over our lines S.E. of WIELTJE. Fired at by Anti-aircraft machine guns. Capt Dann (attd. left to join 182 Coy) J.H.R.	
	28.5.17		The enemy raided our lines after a small bombardment at 3.30 am. All guns opened on S.O.S lines. During night ten guns fired upon targets selected. Ammunition expended 55,750 rounds. JHR	

2449 Wt. W14957/M90 750,000 1/16 J.B.C. & A. Forms/C.2118/12.

Army Form C. 2118.

Instructions regarding War Diaries and Intelligence Summaries are contained in F. S. Regs., Part II. and the Staff Manual respectively. Title Pages will be prepared in manuscript.

WAR DIARY
or
INTELLIGENCE SUMMARY

(Erase heading not required.)

117 M.G. Company

Place	Date	Hour	Summary of Events and Information	Remarks and references to Appendices
HILL TOP SECTOR	29.5.17		Enemy shelled MONMOUTH TRENCH between 5.30 p.m and 6.30 p.m with 4.2 shells and medium trench mortars. Hostile machine guns active over HILL TOP region Lt GARNHAM H.E } Reinforcements 2Lt DONOVAN W.P } 1 O.R to C.C.S. J.H.R.	
"	30.5.17		Relieved in the line by the 116 Coy M.G.C. Company then proceed to "D" Camp into rest billets. 1. O.R. transfered from 118 Coy M.G.C. J.H.R.	
"	31.5.17		Training in rest billets. J.H.R	

C. Menard Major
117 Coy. M.G.C

2449 Wt. W14957/M90 750,000 1/16 J.B.C. & A. Forms/C.2118/12.

Army Form C. 2118.

Instructions regarding War Diaries and Intelligence Summaries are contained in F. S. Regs., Part II. and the Staff Manual respectively. Title Pages will be prepared in manuscript.

WAR DIARY
or
~~INTELLIGENCE SUMMARY~~
(Erase heading not required.)

117th Machine Gun Coy.

117 Coy. M.G.C.

Vol 14

Place	Date	Hour	Summary of Events and Information	Remarks and references to Appendices
"D" CAMP	1.6.17		Training in rest Billets J.H.R.	
"	2.6.17		" " " " J.H.R.	
"	3.6.17		" " " " J.H.R.	
"	4.6.17		" " " " J.H.R.	
"	5.6.17		" " " " J.H.R	
"	6.6.17		" " " J.H.R	
"	7.6.17		" " J.H.R	
"S" Camp	8.6.17		" " Company moved to "S" camp. J.H.R.	
"	9.6.17		" " J.H.R	
"	10.6.17		" " " 1.O.R to C.C.S 6.O.R Reinforcements } J.H.R.	
"	11.6.17		" " " J.H.R.	

2449 Wt. W14957/M90 750,000 1/16 J.B.C. & A. Forms/C.2118/12.

Army Form C. 2118.

WAR DIARY
or
INTELLIGENCE SUMMARY
(Erase heading not required.)

Instructions regarding War Diaries and Intelligence Summaries are contained in F. S. Regs., Part II. and the Staff Manual respectively. Title Pages will be prepared in manuscript.

Place	Date	Hour	Summary of Events and Information	Remarks and references to Appendices
S' Camp.	12.6.17		Training in Rest Billets J.H.R. 1. O.R. Reinforcement J.H.R.	
"	13.6.17		Training in Rest Billets 2. O.R. reinforcements J.H.R.	
"	14.6.17		" " " " 1. O.R. C.C.S.	
HILL TOP SECTOR	15.6.17		Coy relieved the 116 Coy in the HILL TOP SECTOR.	
"	16.6.17		St JEAN was heavily shelled by the enemy from 6.15 p.m to 7.15 p.m. Two enemy aeroplanes flew over our lines between 5 + 6 a.m. Engaged by anti-aircraft machine guns. 2. O.R. to C.C.S. 2/Lt MONTAGUE A.C. killed in action J.H.R.	
"	17.6.17		Clifford Towers position shelled at intervals throughout the day. Coney Street intermittently shelled. LA BELLE ALLIANCE heavily shelled between 8 and 11 p.m. FOCH FARM continuously shelled throughout the morning. Enemy aeroplanes active over front lines during early hours of morning. 1. O.R to C.C.S. J.H.R.	

2449 Wt. W14957/M90 750,000 1/16 J.B.C. & A. Forms/C.2118/12.

Army Form C. 2118.

Instructions regarding War Diaries and Intelligence Summaries are contained in F. S. Regs., Part II. and the Staff Manual respectively. Title Pages will be prepared in manuscript.

WAR DIARY
or
~~INTELLIGENCE SUMMARY~~

(Erase heading not required.)

117 Coy. M.G.C.

Place	Date	Hour	Summary of Events and Information	Remarks and references to Appendices
HILLTOP SECTOR	18.6.17		Enemy shelled the following places during the early hours of the morning. WILSON FARM. IRISH FARM. LA BRIQUE. Enemy aeroplanes active over our front system during the morning and evening. J.H.R.	
"	19.6.17		Enemy artillery very active. Positions in vicinity of LA BELLE ALLIANCE shelled continuously throughout the day and night. Enemy aeroplanes active over our lines at 6 a.m. and in the evening at 9 p.m. Engaged by machine guns J.H.R.	
"	20.6.17		Enemy shelled HILLTOP during the night. Gas shells were used by the enemy on area between LA BRIQUE and DEAD END, between 12 midnight and 1.30 a.m. LA BELLE ALLIANCE and FOCH FARM shelled during the morning. Enemy aeroplanes active during early morning and in the afternoon. Engaged by machine guns J.H.R.	

2449 Wt. W14957/M90 750,000 1/16 J.B.C. & A. Forms/C.2118/12.

Instructions regarding War Diaries and Intelligence Summaries are contained in F. S. Regs., Part II. and the Staff Manual respectively. Title Pages will be prepared in manuscript.

WAR DIARY
or
INTELLIGENCE SUMMARY
(Erase heading not required.)

Army Form C. 2118.

117 Coy. M.G.C.

Place	Date	Hour	Summary of Events and Information	Remarks and references to Appendices
HILLTOP SECTOR	21.6.17		Hostile artillery active on the following positions HILL TOP 2.30 p.m. WILSON FARM 1.30 a.m. 2.30 a.m. gas shells LA BELLE ALLIANCE Intermittently One bomb dropped by enemy aeroplane over junction BOAR LANE + COVEY St. Enemy aeroplanes active over front system from 6 a.m to 7 a.m. Engaged by machine guns. 1. O.R. wounded - admitted F.A. G.H.R.	
"	22.6.17		Enemy shelled the following positions during the night. LA BELLE ALLIANCE WILSON FARM HILL TOP DAWSON CITY BILGE TRENCH Enemy aeroplanes active over front system during the following hours 3.40 a.m to 5 a.m. G.H.R.	

2449 Wt. W14957/M90 750,000 1/16 J.B.C. & A. Forms/C.2118/12.

Army Form C. 2118.

Instructions regarding War Diaries and Intelligence Summaries are contained in F. S. Regs., Part II. and the Staff Manual respectively. Title Pages will be prepared in manuscript.

WAR DIARY
or
~~INTELLIGENCE SUMMARY~~

(Erase heading not required.)

117 Coy M G C

Place	Date	Hour	Summary of Events and Information	Remarks and references to Appendices
HILL TOP SECTOR	23.6.17		Enemy artillery active. The following positions shelled at varying intervals. LA BELLE ALLIANCE LONE WILLOW WILSON FARM THREADNEEDLE STR.	
			Enemy aeroplane activity below normal. One plane seen at 4 a.m. Engaged by machine guns	
			LT. CROCKATT. D. reinforcement JHR	
	24.6.17		Enemy artillery active. The following positions were shelled at varying intervals BILGE TR. WILSON FARM IRISH FARM.	
			Usual enemy aeroplane activity over front line system. Engaged by machine guns. JHR	

2449 Wt. W14957/M90 750,000 1/16 J.B.C. & A. Forms/C.2118/12.

Army Form C. 2118.

WAR DIARY
or
INTELLIGENCE SUMMARY
(Erase heading not required.)

117 Coy M.G.C.

Instructions regarding War Diaries and Intelligence Summaries are contained in F. S. Regs., Part II. and the Staff Manual respectively. Title Pages will be prepared in manuscript.

Place	Date	Hour	Summary of Events and Information	Remarks and references to Appendices
HILLTOP SECTOR	25.6.17		Enemy shelled the following positions throughout the night. BILGE TRENCH THREADNEEDLE STR. WILSON FARM 11 p.m to 11.45 p.m. Our artillery opened from 1 a.m to 1.20 a.m causing the enemy to put up red and green lights Usual early morning enemy aircraft activity. Engaged by machine guns. One hostile plane brought down by our planes. 1. O.R. wounded - admitted F.A. G.H.R.	
"	26.6.17		Enemy shelled the following places. Heavily shelled at the times stated. CONEY STR. BOAR LANE. 2 p.m. 4 30 p.m. WILSON FM 11.30 a.m to 1.30 p.m. IRISH FM 2.30 a.m BILGE TRENCH 1.15 a.m to 1.45 a.m 2.30 a.m to 3.15 a.m. THREADNEEDLE ST. 6.30 p.m to 7 p.m. Enemy aeroplanes active over front system. engaged by machine guns G.H.R.	

2449 Wt. W14957/M90 750,000 1/16 J.B.C. & A. Forms/C.2118/12.

Army Form C. 2118.

Instructions regarding War Diaries and Intelligence Summaries are contained in F. S. Regs., Part II. and the Staff Manual respectively. Title Pages will be prepared in manuscript.

WAR DIARY
or
~~INTELLIGENCE SUMMARY~~
(Erase heading not required.)

117 Coy M.G.C.

Place	Date	Hour	Summary of Events and Information	Remarks and references to Appendices
HILL TOP SECTOR	27.6.17.		Enemy shelled WILSON FARM from 11.30 pm throughout the night. HILL TOP was heavily shelled by 4.2 s from 9.30 p.m to 12.30 am. Entrance to HILL TOP REDOUBT from CONEY STREET blocked by two direct hits on the trench. 1 a.m to 2 a.m minor artillery bombardment to the left of Bde Sector. JHR	
"	28.6.17		Enemy used tear gas shells on the trench junction CONEY STREET – BOAR LANE during the night. Enemy artillery and trench mortars active on HILL TOP AREA. Three direct hits were observed on the small trench leading to VIEW FARM EMPLACEMENT	
"	29.6.17		Enemy shelled the following places LA BRIQUE WILSON FM IRISH FARM CONEY ST. CANAL BANK 1 O.R. killed 2 O.R. wounded. JHR.	

2449 Wt. W14957/M90 750,000 1/16 J.B.C. & A. Forms/C.2118/12.

Army Form C. 2118.

WAR DIARY
or
INTELLIGENCE SUMMARY

(Erase heading not required.)

Instructions regarding War Diaries and Intelligence Summaries are contained in F. S. Regs., Part II. and the Staff Manual respectively. Title Pages will be prepared in manuscript.

117 Coy M.G.C.

Place	Date	Hour	Summary of Events and Information	Remarks and references to Appendices
HILLTOP SECTOR	30.6.17		Company relieved on night of 29/30 by 113 Machine Gun Company. Coy then proceeded to "C" camp. JHR.	

C Renardhuys
O.C. 117th M.G.C.

2449 Wt. W14957/M90 750,000 1/16 J.B.C. & A. Forms/C.2118/12.

Army Form C. 2118.

Instructions regarding War Diaries and Intelligence Summaries are contained in F. S. Regs., Part II. and the Staff Manual respectively. Title pages will be prepared in manuscript.

WAR DIARY
or
~~INTELLIGENCE SUMMARY.~~ 117 Coy M.G.C.

(Erase heading not required.)

MC/15

Place	Date	Hour	Summary of Events and Information	Remarks and references to Appendices
"C" Camp.	1.7.17		Training in Rest Billets J.H.R Coy proceeded to SALPERWICK AREA J.H.R.	
SALPERWICK	2.7.17		Training in Rest Billets J.H.R.	
"	3.7.17		" " " One O.R to England on munitions J.H.R.	
"	4.7.17		" " " J.H.R	
"	5.7.17		" " " J.H.R.	
"	6.7.17		" " " MAJOR JERRARD and 1.O.R. transferred to 66 Div. J.H.R	
"	7.7.17		" " " J.H.R.	
"	8.7.17		" " " 1. O.R transferred to 116 M.G Coy. J.H.R.	
"	9.7.17		" " " CAPT. RASTEUR and 1 O.R. from 51st M.G Coy J.H.R.	
"	10.7.17		" " " J.H.R.	
"	11.7.17		" " " 1 O.R joined from CCS J.H.R.	
"	12.7.17		" " " J.H.R.	

A5834 Wt. W4973/M687 750,000 8/16 D. D. & L. Ltd. Forms/C.2118/13.

Army Form C. 2118.

WAR DIARY
~~or~~
~~INTELLIGENCE SUMMARY.~~ 117 M.G. Coy
(*Erase heading not required.*)

Instructions regarding War Diaries and Intelligence Summaries are contained in F. S. Regs., Part II. and the Staff Manual respectively. Title pages will be prepared in manuscript.

Place	Date	Hour	Summary of Events and Information	Remarks and references to Appendices
SALPERWICK	13.7.17		Training in Rest Billets J.H.R	
"	14.7.17		" " " " J.H.R	
"	15.7.17		" " " " J.H.R	
"	16.7.17		" " " " J.H.R	
"	17.7.17		" " " " 1.O.R. Reinforcement from base. J.H.R	
"	18.7.17		" " " " 1.O.R. Evacuated J.H.R.	
"	19.7.17		" " " " J.H.R	
"	20.7.17		" " " " 1.O.R. Evacuated J.H.R.	
"	21.7.17		Coy moved to A.30 Camps. 3.O.R evacuated J.H.R	
A.30 Camp	22.7.17		Training in Rest Billets 2.O.R evacuated J.H.R.	
"	23.7.17		" " " " 1.O.R evacuated J.H.R.	
"	24.7.17		" " " " J.H.R.	
"	25.7.17		" " " " 1.O.R evacuated J.H.R	

A5834 Wt. W4973/M687 750,000 8/16 D. D. & L. Ltd. Forms/C.2118/13.

WAR DIARY

or ~~INTELLIGENCE SUMMARY.~~ 117 Coy M.G.C.

(*Erase heading not required.*)

Army Form C. 2118.

Instructions regarding War Diaries and Intelligence Summaries are contained in F. S. Regs., Part II. and the Staff Manual respectively. Title pages will be prepared in manuscript.

Place	Date	Hour	Summary of Events and Information	Remarks and references to Appendices
A.30 CAMP	26.7.17		Training in Rest Billets J.H.R.	
"	27.7.17		" " " J.H.R.	
"	28.7.17		" " " " J.H.R.	
"	29.7.17		Coy moved to CANAL BANK. 1.O.R to Hosp. Sick J.H.R.	
HILL TOP SECTOR	30.7.17		Coy moved to assembly positions in HILL TOP SECTOR on night of 30/31 July. Owing to hostile shelling two guns were put out of action with the following casualties. CASUALTIES DURING ASSEMBLY 2 O.Rs KILLED 6 O.Rs WOUNDED.	
"	31.7.17		At Zero hour the Company took part in a general attack by the Fifth Army. Eight guns were told off to consolidate and eight guns to do barrage work. (See appendix 1.) All guns moved forward at zero according to instructions. Lt SUTHERLAND (BLACK LINE) carried on with two guns. One gun team, being unable to get in touch with 2Lt DONOVAN carried on alone towards its objective. This gun was taken in hand by Lt SUTHERLAND and used in addition to his two guns, to consolidate the dotted BLACK LINE, and placed at the left edge of KITCHENER'S WOOD. Later 2Lt BELL took this gun forward to REGINA CROSS ROADS. The barrage guns arrived in position in vicinity of	See Appendix 1.

A5834 Wt. W4973/M687 750,000 8/16 D. D. & L. Ltd. Forms/C.2118/13.

Instructions regarding War Diaries and Intelligence Summaries are contained in F. S. Regs., Part II. and the Staff Manual respectively. Title pages will be prepared in manuscript.

WAR DIARY
or
INTELLIGENCE SUMMARY.
(Erase heading not required.)

Army Form C. 2118.

Place	Date	Hour	Summary of Events and Information	Remarks and references to Appendices
			KULTUR FARM by Z+2 hrs. Only six guns of the eight detailed were able to fire, owing to one gun being put out of action and one being sent forward to reinforce the BLACK LINE. This gun met with heavy shell fire going round the right side of KITCHENERS WOOD. After the tripod and some of the gun numbers had been "knocked out", the N.C.O in charge reported back to the BLUE LINE.	
			The barrage guns moved forward to fire the second barrage from "C" positions at Z+ 6 hrs 20 mins. One gun and team was put out of action on the way, thus only five guns fired from the 'C' position. It was found impossible to fire from the positions previously chosen owing to the consolidation of the BLACK LINE and the excessive movement in front of the guns. Positions were then chosen in front of the dotted BLACK LINE and the barrage fired from there. Two hours after the cessation of the barrage three guns moved back to the BLUE LINE in reserve, and two guns under 2nd Lt PLAYFAIR remained to reinforce the BLACK LINE. While the barrage was being fired a gun of 2nd Lt SUTHERLAND'S was put out of action. An unsuccessful attempt was made to replace it by a gun from the BLUE LINE, which returned after meeting excessive shell fire minus a tripod. At Z+12 hrs Lt CROCKATT with one gun and team proceeded to reinforce the BLACK LINE and Lt CROCKATT took command of the defence of the BLACK LINE, Lt SUTHERLAND having become a casualty.	
			On the evening of the 31st of July the dispositions of the guns were as follows	

Army Form C. 2118.

Instructions regarding War Diaries and Intelligence Summaries are contained in F. S. Regs., Part II. and the Staff Manual respectively. Title pages will be prepared in manuscript.

WAR DIARY
or
INTELLIGENCE SUMMARY.
(Erase heading not required.)

Place	Date	Hour	Summary of Events and Information	Remarks and references to Appendices
			2 guns REGINA CROSS ROADS 4 " BLACK LINE 4 " BLUE LINE 3 guns in reserve two of which were minus tripods. A steady rain set in ~~during~~ during the evening but consolidation was continued energetically till dawn. During this period the main shelling of the BLACK LINE area fell on the front and rear edges of KITCHENER'S WOOD and the CANOE SYSTEM. CASUALTIES MACHINE GUN CORPS 2LT PLAYFAIR wounded Lt SUTHERLAND " 6. O.R. killed 14 O.R. wounded. ATTACHED MEN. 3. O.R. killed 12. O.R. wounded 2. O.R. missing. J.M.R. [signature] Capt. O/C 117. M.G. Coy	

A5834 Wt. W4973/M687 750,000 8/16 D. D. & L. Ltd. Forms/C.2118/13.

Instructions regarding War Diaries and Intelligence Summaries are contained in F. S. Regs., Part II. and the Staff Manual respectively. Title pages will be prepared in manuscript.

WAR DIARY
or
~~INTELLIGENCE SUMMARY.~~
(Erase heading not required.)

117th M. Gun Coy

Vol 16

Army Form C. 2118.

Place	Date	Hour	Summary of Events and Information	Remarks and references to Appendices
HILLTOP SECTOR	1.8.17		The right BLACK LINE gun was knocked out at 3.30 pm. Excessive shelling in this area from 2.30 to 3.35 pm. Continuous rain throughout the day. Trenches flooded out. BLACK LINE relief in on the night 1st/2nd. On the same night two teams were sent up to ALBERTA & the guns were so disposed to defend the the right flank, which had become exposed owing to the successive withdrawals of 116 & 118 Bdes. The disposition of the guns was therefore 2 guns at REGINA CROSS RDS 3 guns in BLACK LINE 2 " " ALBERTA. 2 " " BLUE LINE 3 " " Reserve.	
	2.8.17		Continuous rain. The whole country now a morass. BLACK LINE flooded out & moved forward on the right company front of the 117 Bde front to ALBERTA strong point. Two of the BLACK LINE guns moved forward with this company.	
	3.8.17		Left gun of BLACK LINE moved forward to ADAMS FM.	

A5834 Wt. W4973/M687 750,000 8/16 D. D. & L. Ltd. Forms/C.2118/13.

Instructions regarding War Diaries and Intelligence Summaries are contained in F. S. Regs., Part II. and the Staff Manual respectively. Title pages will be prepared in manuscript.

WAR DIARY
or
INTELLIGENCE SUMMARY.
(*Erase heading not required.*)

Army Form C. 2118.

Place	Date	Hour	Summary of Events and Information	Remarks and references to Appendices
3	3.8.17		Team sent up 24 hours previous to reinforce the BLACK LINE joined the teams in ALBERTA.	
			One gun at ALBERTA used for antiaircraft work fired several times at aeroplanes flying low.	
			Showery but not continuous rain.	
			2 BLUE LINE guns & 2 from reserve relieved 8 guns of 116 Company in CANOPUS TRENCH.	
			Disposition of guns was then:—	
			2 guns in REGINA X RDS.	
			5 guns in ALBERTA (3 for defence of BLACK LINE & 2 for defence of right flank)	
			1 gun in ADAMS FM for defence of BLACK LINE	
			4 guns in CANOPUS TRENCH.	
	4.8.17		Much shelling of BLACK LINE & ALBERTA area	
			Weather comparatively fine	
			Intense shelling later on in the night.	
	5.8.17		Weather cleared to bright sunshine.	
			1 team sent to Coy HQ from ALBERTA to be in reserve	
			Night of 5th/6th whole Company relieved & went to rest camp at REIGERSBURG CHATEAU.	

A5834 Wt. W4973/M687 750,000 8/16 D. D. & L. Ltd. Forms/C.2118/13.

Army Form C. 2118.

Instructions regarding War Diaries and Intelligence Summaries are contained in F. S. Regs., Part II. and the Staff Manual respectively. Title pages will be prepared in manuscript.

WAR DIARY
or
~~INTELLIGENCE SUMMARY.~~
(Erase heading not required.)

Vol 21

Place	Date	Hour	Summary of Events and Information	Remarks and references to Appendices
			WAR DIARY 117 COY M.G.C. 1ST JAN — 31 JAN. 1918 (inclusive) [signature] Lt for O.C. 117 Coy Mg C	

A5834 Wt. W4973/M687 750,000 8/16 D. D. & L. Ltd. Forms/C.2118/13.

Instructions regarding War Diaries and Intelligence Summaries are contained in F. S. Regs., Part II. and the Staff Manual respectively. Title pages will be prepared in manuscript.

WAR DIARY
or
INTELLIGENCE SUMMARY.
(Erase heading not required.)

Army Form C. 2118.

Place	Date	Hour	Summary of Events and Information	Remarks and references to Appendices
			Summary of Casualties during period 1st to 6th 1 officer killed 2 OR missing 2 officers wounded 3 OR killed. 11 OR wounded 5 OR to CCS	
	6.8.17		REIGERSBURG CHATEAU in rest.	
METEREN.	7.8.17		trained from VLAMERTINGHE to CAESTRE & then marched to billets in a farm near METEREN.	
	8.8.17		inspection by Divisional & Brigade Commanders	
	9.8.17		cleaning up in billets.	
	10.8.17		inspected by ARMY COMMANDER. 25 OR reinforcements arrived. 2/Lt STEPHENS joins the Company	
	11.8.17		training in billets. 23 OR reinforcements arrived.	
	12.8.17		" " "	
	13.8.17		Coy moved to camp in RIDGE WOOD by bus	
RIDGE WOOD	14.8.17		cleaning up gun equipment	
	15.8.17		" " "	
			On the night 15th/16th Coy relieved 124th M.G. Coy in the sector immediately north of YPRES - COMMINES Canal. Coy HQ in ~~SPOIL BANK~~ BLUFF TUNNELS.	
~~SPOIL BANK~~ BLUFF TUNNELS	16.8.17		5000 rounds fired from B battery (4 guns) - harassing fire.	
	17.8.17		enemy artillery active. Lt. Palmer, Lt Valentine & 2/Lt Rowland joined the company.	

A5834 Wt. W4973/M687 750,000 8/16 D. D. & L. Ltd. Forms/C.2118/13.

Instructions regarding War Diaries and Intelligence Summaries are contained in F. S. Regs., Part II. and the Staff Manual respectively. Title pages will be prepared in manuscript.

WAR DIARY
or
INTELLIGENCE SUMMARY.
(Erase heading not required.)

Army Form C. 2118.

Place	Date	Hour	Summary of Events and Information	Remarks and references to Appendices
	17.8.17		Enemy planes engaged by guns in BATTLE WOOD	
			Heavy shelling of 18 pounder battery near B Battery.	
	18.8.17		CANAL BANK shelled from 10 to 12.30 pm	
			Dump of 30000 rounds SAA formed by pack train at B Battery and a similar dump formed at CATERPILLAR CRATER.	
			New emplacements constructed at CATERPILLAR CRATER	
	19.8.17		Coy relieved on the night 19th/20th by 118 M.G. Coy, and proceeded by march route to RIDGE WOOD.	
RIDGE WOOD	20.8.17		rest and clean up	
	21.8.17		training in camp.	
	22.8.17		night of 22nd/23rd Coy relieved 118 M.G. Coy in the HOLLEBEKE SECTOR. Capt Palmer to hospital - sick	
HOLLEBEKE	23.8.17		Coy HQ shelled in the evening.	
	24.8.17		DAMMSTASSE & wooden road shelled between 10.30 & 12 midnight.	
	25.8.17		Hostile aircraft active near the DAMMSTRASSE. 250 rounds fired.	
	26.8.17		6000 rounds SAA dump created by pack train on the HOLLEBEKE road.	
			Barrage battery position constructed on the right of this road.	
			Normal artillery activity.	
	27.8.17		Heavy rain	
			Artillery activity on the part of the enemy in vicinity of DAMMSTASSE.	
			No aerial activity.	

A5834 Wt. W4973/M687 750,000 8/16 D. D. & L. Ltd. Forms/C.2118/13.

Instructions regarding War Diaries and Intelligence Summaries are contained in F. S. Regs., Part II. and the Staff Manual respectively. Title pages will be prepared in manuscript.

WAR DIARY

or

INTELLIGENCE SUMMARY.

(Erase heading not required.)

Army Form C. 2118.

Place	Date	Hour	Summary of Events and Information	Remarks and references to Appendices
	28.8.17		Coy relieved on night 28th/29th by 63 M.G. Coy, IX Corps, and proceeded to HORRUMBIDGEE camp.	
HORRUMBIDGEE CAMP.	29.8.17 30.8.17		Training in camp	
	31.8.17		2/Lt Goulding joined the company	

Douglas Brockett Lt

117 M.G. Coy. 31-8-1917.

A5834 Wt. W4973/M687 750,000 8/16 D. D. & L. Ltd. Forms/C.2118/13.

SECRET

Operation Order by
Capt H M Pasler
Commdg 117 M G Coy
14th Aug. 1917.

Para I 117th M G Coy will relieve the 124th M G Coy in the Sector immediately north of Ypres-Comines Canal - on the 15th & the night of 15 - 16

Para II All belts S A A maps etc. will be taken over from out-going teams.

Tripods will be taken over at Nos 2. 3. 4 & 5 positions

Gun Posns	Under	Parade Time	Report at Coy H Qs
B Battery	Lt Hasler	5 45 AM.	8 AM.
10 & 17	-do-	-do-	-do-
11 & 18	Lt Rutledge.	7 am.	9 am.
Coy H Qs	O.C.	7 am	9 am.
7. 8 & 9.	2/Lt Bell.	5 pm	7 pm
4 & 5	" Stevens.	5 30 pm.	7 30 pm.
12 & 13	Sgt Riley [illegible]	5 30 p.m	7.30 p.m.

The route to be taken in all cases will be via VOORMEZEELE & wooden track to Coy Dump where limbers are to be unpacked thence to Coy Hdqrs.

Transport lines will remain at /

at present Q. M. Stores at Transport lines

5. Runners will be provided from Sectionals & Company Headquarters

(1) One each from 10 & 17 Gun teams

(2) One each to proceed with No 11 & 18 Gun teams

(3) Two to proceed with 2 & 3 gun teams & two with 8 and 9 gun teams

(4) Two to proceed with 4 & 5 gun team

All runners will return to Company Headquarters immediately after relief.

(6) WATER

In case of emergency water can be drawn from Brigade Headqrs SOIL BANK in exchange for empty tins

Water can also be obtained as follows

(1) From well 1 33 a 40 10

(2) " spring 0 4 b 10 50

Water cart refilling point

1 31 d 20 45

7. SAA

Main Brigade Dump at Bluff Tunnels

Advanced Dump HEDGE ROW

do - do CORD LANE

8 MEDICAL

RAP at I 36 c 20 10

I 35 central.

Collecting Post I 38 d 30 60

9 SOCKS Clean dry socks will be provided but only in exchange for dirty pairs. These will be returned with ration parties each night

10 HOT FOOD

Every effort will be made to provide hot meals in cases where teams are unable to cook

11 TRENCH STORE LIST

Lists of stores taken over will be sent down by runners returning from teams immediately after the relief.

12 RATIONS

With the exception of "B" Battery guns rations will be sent up by means of runners + spare men. No ration parties will therefore be required

[illegible] Capt.

O/C 114 M.G. Coy.

9.30 pm.

14th

Operation Order No. 8
by Capt. F. M. PASTEUR
Comdg. 117th Machine Gun Company

SECRET.

Ref. Map Sheet 28 [illegible] 2½0,000.

1. The Coy. will relieve 118th Machine Gun Company on the 22nd and night of 22/23rd in the HOLLEBEKE Sector.

2. Relief will be complete by 3 a.m.

3. Distribution of Guns.
(a) No. 1 Section. 1, 2 and 3 positions and one gun at Coy. Hdqrs.
(b) No. 3 Section. 4, 5 and 6 positions and one gun at Coy. Hdqrs.
(c) No. 4 Section. 4 guns barrage positions
(d) No. 2 Section. 4 guns anti-aircraft positions in ST. ELOI Craters.

4. March Route and Guides

Section	Starting time	Route	Meet guides at	Time to meet guides
No. 1	2.55 p.m.	Cross Roads N.6.a.10.15. MONMOUTH ROAD & BUS HO. O.2.a.30.70. OOSTHOEK Estaminet O.3.d.0.0.	BUS HO. O.2.a.30.70.	4 p.m.
No. 2	1.30 p.m.	" to ST. ELOI Craters	No guides	—
No. 3	1.55 p.m.	Cross Roads N.6.a.10.15. MONMOUTH ROAD & BUS HO. O.2.a.30.70. OOSTHOEK Estaminet O.3.d.0.0.	BUS HO. O.2.a.70.30	3 p.m.
No. 4	1.30 p.m.	Cross roads N.6.a.10.15 & MONMOUTH ROAD	On MONMOUTH ROAD 250 yards short of Briquetterie near SPOIL BANK	3 p.m.

5. Guides meeting Sections at Bus House will take them to Coy. Hdqrs. where there will be guides for each position.

6. Rations and Water.
Unconsumed portion of the day's ration will be carried on the person. Rations for the 23rd inst. will accompany sections on transport. Water bottles will be filled and inspected by section officers before starting. 2 full petrol tins will be left in each position. Water supply will be organised from Company Headquarters.

7. Belt boxes, S.A.A., maps, 2 petrol tins per position and any other trench stores will be taken over. Duplicate receipts will be sent to Company Headquarters.

8. Relief complete will be reported to Company Headquarters.

9. Company Headquarters will be at O.4.c.15.20

Copies issued
C.O.
4 Sections
Transport Officer
C.S.M.
C.Q.M.S.
117th Infantry Bde.
War Diary

[illegible] Pasteur. Capt
[illegible] 117 M.G. Coy

Received 21st [illegible]

Instructions regarding War Diaries and Intelligence Summaries are contained in F. S. Regs., Part II, and the Staff Manual respectively. Title pages will be prepared in manuscript.

WAR DIARY

or

~~INTELLIGENCE SUMMARY.~~

(*Erase heading not required.*)

Army Form C. 2118.

Vol 17

Place	Date	Hour	Summary of Events and Information	Remarks and references to Appendices
			CONFIDENTIAL	
			WAR DIARY.	
			1 SEPT. —— 30 SEPT. 1917 (inclusive)	
			117 COY. MACHINE GUN CORPS	
			[signature] Lt. / A/O.C. / 117 Coy M.G.C.	

A5834 Wt. W4973/M687 750,000 8/16 D. D. & L. Ltd. Forms/C.2118/13.

Instructions regarding War Diaries and Intelligence Summaries are contained in F. S. Regs., Part II. and the Staff Manual respectively. Title pages will be prepared in manuscript.

WAR DIARY
or
INTELLIGENCE SUMMARY.
(Erase heading not required.)

Army Form C. 2118.

Place	Date	Hour	Summary of Events and Information	Remarks and references to Appendices
MORRUMBIDGEE CAMP	1/9/17		Inspection by Brigadier General Commanding	
	2/9/17		Training in camp	
	3/9/17		" " "	
	4/9/17		Company proceeded by march route to billets in STEENVOORD area	
	5/9/17		Training in billets	
	6/9/17		" " "	
	7/9/17		" " "	
	8/9/17		" " "	
	9/9/17		" " "	
	10/9/17		" " "	
RIDGE WOOD	11/9/17		Company moved to RIDGE WOOD.	
			Night 11/12 5 guns relieved 5 guns of 116 M.G. Coy in LARCH WOOD SECTOR.	
	12/9/17		Remainder of company relieved the remainder of 116 M.G. Coy in the LARCH WOOD SECTOR	
LARCH WOOD	13/9/17		Enemy aeroplanes very active. 1250 rounds were fired at them in all, chiefly by the LARCH WOOD & MT. SORREL Guns	
			Time spent chiefly in sections doing assembly positions	
			New emplacement constructed at S4 position.	
	14/9/17		Company relieved by 116 M.G. Coy and proceeded by march route to RIDGE WOOD Camp.	
RIDGE WOOD	15/9/17		Company moved from RIDGE WOOD to camp in MILLEKRUISSE area	

A5834 Wt. W4973/M687 750,000 8/16 D. D. & L. Ltd. Forms/C.2118/13.

Army Form C. 2118.

Instructions regarding War Diaries and Intelligence Summaries are contained in F. S. Regs., Part II. and the Staff Manual respectively. Title pages will be prepared in manuscript.

WAR DIARY
or
INTELLIGENCE SUMMARY.

(Erase heading not required.)

Place	Date	Hour	Summary of Events and Information	Remarks and references to Appendices
MILLEKRUISSE AREA	16/9/17		Training in camp	
"	17/9/17		" " " Lieut. Platts transferred from 116 Coy. with appointment of 2nd in Command took over command of the Coy	JHP
"	18/9/17		" " During the night the 118 Coy. took over the Camp and the Coy. bivouaced in the open.	JHP
	19/9/17		Final preparations made for the attack on the following morning. Coy. moved up to its assembly positions in the RAVINE by march route. Practically no shelling to interfere with this.	JHP
THE RAVINE & (BULGAR WOOD)	20/9/17		Assembly reported complete by 4.20 a.m. Guns were detailed as follows:–	JHP
			8 guns to the RED LINE, 2 of these were to move forward to the GREEN LINE when that objective was captured.	
			6 guns to the BLUE LINE, 2 of these guns were operating on the front of the Bde. on the right.	
			2 guns in Reserve at Coy. H. Q. in the RAVINE.	
			Before the Assembly was complete one of the BLUE LINE guns had become a casualty with one gunner, this gun was replaced by one of the Reserve guns from Coy. H.Q.S.	
			The whole moved forward at Zero, 5.40 a.m. the RED LINE was reached without difficulty, and the 8 guns detailed for this portion of the defence got into position on roughly a line running N. & S. just E. of the CUTTING, (200x E. of KINGS CASTLE and JULES FM.)	
			One of these guns was put out of action by shellfire shortly after arriving in position	

A5834 Wt. W4973/M687 750,000 8/16 D. D. & L. Ltd. Forms/C.2118/13.

Instructions regarding War Diaries and Intelligence Summaries are contained in F. S. Regs., Part II. and the Staff Manual respectively. Title pages will be prepared in manuscript.

WAR DIARY
or
INTELLIGENCE SUMMARY.
(Erase heading not required.)

Army Form C. 2118.

Place	Date	Hour	Summary of Events and Information	Remarks and references to Appendices
THE RAVINE (+ BULGAR WOOD)	cont 20/9/17		Of the 6 Blue Lines Guns, the two on the front of the Bde. on the right kept close up to the Infantry and got into position at TOP HOUSE. These two guns were of great assistance in the capture of a German M.G. which was holding up the advance in this region, as they were able to open fire on it & enabling the infantry to work round to a flank & capture it. Of the remaining four detailed for the BLUE LINE, the two guns on the left followed up the infantry rather too closely the result being that the Guns detachments became engaged in hand to hand fighting. This ended by one gun being put out of action and the officer in charge of the pair being killed (Lieut Palmer). The remaining gun of this pair got into action slightly in rear of the BLUE LINE but had worked across too far to the right. The remaining two guns not yet mentioned, detailed for the BLUE LINE were too slow in moving from the vicinity of the RED LINE they, however, moved up into position during the late afternoon, one of the pair being knocked out on the move forward.	
			At 9 a.m. the situation not being very clear, the left flank of the Bde being somewhat exposed on account of the Division on the left not having made the progress they intended, the two RED LINE guns detailed for the defence of the GREE LINE + the one remaining reserve gun at Coy H.Q. were ordered to push	

A5834 Wt. W4973/M687 750,000 8/16 D. D. & L. Ltd. Forms/C.2118/13.

Army Form C. 2118.

Instructions regarding War Diaries and Intelligence Summaries are contained in F. S. Regs., Part II. and the Staff Manual respectively. Title pages will be prepared in manuscript.

WAR DIARY
or
INTELLIGENCE SUMMARY.

(Erase heading not required.)

Place	Date	Hour	Summary of Events and Information	Remarks and references to Appendices
THE RAVINE + BULGAR WOOD	cont 20/9/17		forward to the vicinity of the BLUE LINE and make the left flank of the Bde secure. This they did by getting into position on the forward slope of the ground running down towards the BASSEVILLEBEEK. These guns engaged several targets and were very helpful in the consolidation + digging in process, as they were able to bring direct overhead fire to bear on the enemy positions. The position on the night of the 20th was as follows:– 7 guns in the BLUE LINE (2 guns on the rt + 3 on left being pushed well forward close up to + in the BLUE LINE) 5 guns in the RED LINE. (The remaining 4 of the Coy having been knocked out). The night passed quietly.	
"	21/9/17		From 10 a.m. till late in the afternoon the enemy carefully registered and ranged. At 5.30 p.m. the 118th Coy. arrived to relieve the Coy. At 7 p.m. the S.O.S. went up on both sides, and a heavy bombardment ensued lasting till 9 p.m. The barrage put down by the enemy during this period was the heaviest + most severe of the battle. Incoming teams suffered as a result. Relief was reported complete by 11.20 p.m. The Coy moved into camp at RIDGE WOOD.	JMP.

A5834 Wt. W4973/M687 750,000 8/16 D. D. & L. Ltd. Forms/C.2118/13.

WAR DIARY
or
INTELLIGENCE SUMMARY.
(Erase heading not required.)

Army Form C. 2118.

Instructions regarding War Diaries and Intelligence Summaries are contained in F. S. Regs., Part II. and the Staff Manual respectively. Title pages will be prepared in manuscript.

Place	Date	Hour	Summary of Events and Information	Remarks and references to Appendices
RIDGEWOOD	26/9/17		Day spent in rest. Preparations made for moving into line early morning following	JRCP
CLONNEL COPSE	27/9/17		Coy. moved up to line by march route leaving RIDGE WOOD at 6.45 a.m. met guides JACKSON'S DUMP at 8.0 p.m. Relieved 123 Coy. M.G.C. in A & B M.G. battery positions just S. of CLONNEL COPSE. Relief complete by 10.15 a.m. At 6.47 p.m. S.O.S. went up on the left followed by 1 on our front. Coy fired 25,000 Rds on to S.O.S. lines, everything quite by dark (The section detailed for A.A. work moved up with the Coy to CLONNEL COPSE)	JRCP
CLONNEL COPSE	28/9/17		Coy relieved at 2.15 p.m. by 247 M.G. Coy. (37 Div) with 8 guns, remaining 8 gun positions vacated. Coy collected at BUS HOUSE at 4.30 p.m. lorried from here to LOCRE. Reinforcements 2/Lieut McSwan & 2nd Lieut. Tight	JRCP
LOCRE	29/9/17		Cleaning up of gun kit, attention to belts etc	JRCP
LOCRE	30/9/17		Inspection by Divisional General. Attached men rejoin their units.	JRCP

J.R.C. Platt Lieut
A/O.C. 117 Coy Machine Gun Corps

Army Form C. 2118.

WAR DIARY
or
INTELLIGENCE SUMMARY.
(Erase heading not required.)

Instructions regarding War Diaries and Intelligence Summaries are contained in F. S. Regs., Part II. and the Staff Manual respectively. Title pages will be prepared in manuscript.

Place	Date	Hour	Summary of Events and Information	Remarks and references to Appendices
RIDGE WOOD	21/9/17		The Coy went into the battle with 10 officers and 155 O.Rs and 16 guns. It came out with 7 officers and 120 O.Rs (Lieut Palmer killed, Lieut Kirkby died of wounds, Lieut Rutledge wounded) and 15 guns. Three of the latter being unserviceable. The day was spent in resting and cleaning up. At 10 p.m. the Coy embussed at the BRASSERIE and proceeded to ASCOT CAMP, WESTOUTRE. arrived midnight JMP	
ASCOT CAMP WESTOUTRE	22/9/17		Day spent in cleaning up gun kit etc JMP	
"	23/9/17		Making up deficiencies JMP	
"	24/9/17		Cleaning Belts, reloading same & preparing generally for the line. 50 O.Rs reinforcements arrived. At 8.45 p.m. the Coy accompanied by its limbers proceeded by march route to RIDGE WOOD, arrived about midnight. One section proceeded on from here to the line to take up A.A. positions in the OBSERVATORY RIDGE sector, 2 guns at KNOWLE FM. and 2 at MT. SORREL. They were in position by 5.30 a.m. (25th inst) JMP.	
RIDGE WOOD	25/9/17		Coy. in Divisional Reserve. Day spent in rest. JMP	

A5834 Wt. W4973/M687 750,000 8/16 D. D. & L. Ltd. Forms/C.2118/13.

Instructions regarding War Diaries and Intelligence Summaries are contained in F. S. Regs., Part II. and the Staff Manual respectively. Title pages will be prepared in manuscript.

WAR DIARY
or
INTELLIGENCE SUMMARY.
(*Erase heading not required.*)

OCT 17

117th M.G. Coy

Vol 18

Army Form C. 2118.

Place	Date 1917	Hour	Summary of Events and Information	Remarks and references to Appendices
LOCRE	1 Oct.		Training in vicinity of Camp. 2nd Lieut WREN from base joined the Coy	JHP
"	2 "		Training in vicinity of Camp	JHP
"	3		" " "	JHP
"	4 "		" " " JHP	
"	5 "		" " " JHP	
"	6 "		" " " JHP	
"	7 "		Voluntary Church Services JHP	
"	8 "		Training in vicinity of Camp JHP	
"	9 "		" " " " JHP	
"	10 "		" " " " JHP	
"	11 "		" " " " Lieut WHITBY transferred from 206 Coy M.G.C. assumed Command	JHP
"	12		" " " " " JHP	
"	13		" " " " " JHP	
"	14		" " " " " JHP An Advance party of 4 men + Lieut Crockett proceeded to WILLEBEEK CAMP.	JHP
"	15		The Coy. left its quarters in LOCRE at 3.30 p.m and proceeded by march route to WILLEBEEK CAMP via CANADA CORNER – HALLEBAST – CONFUSION CORNER Map Ref N9d 7.5. The Coy. was in its quarters by 6.0 p.m. Some hostile planes passed overhead during early part of night and drew a good deal of A.A. fire. Bombs could be heard exploding in the distance JHP	Reference Map Belgium + France Sheet 28 and SHREWSBURY FOREST

Army Form C. 2118.

WAR DIARY
or
INTELLIGENCE SUMMARY.
(Erase heading not required.)

Instructions regarding War Diaries and Intelligence Summaries are contained in F. S. Regs., Part II. and the Staff Manual respectively. Title pages will be prepared in manuscript.

Place	Date 1917	Hour	Summary of Events and Information	Remarks and references to Appendices
WILLEBEEK CAMP N9 d 7.5.	OCT 16		½ Coy training. ½ Coy relieved 111 Coy at Barrage Positions in the TOWER HAMLETS Sector 'A' Batty (4 guns) at J25 a 6.3. 'B' Batty (4 guns) at J25 b 3.4	[initials]
"	OCT 17 18 19		½ Coy in line as above. ½ Coy training at WILLEBEEK CAMP.	[initials]
SHREWSBURY FOREST SECTOR	OCT. 20		118 Coy relieved Barrage guns of 117 Coy Coy relieved guns of 116 Coy distributed as follows in the SHREWSBURY FOREST Sector J group - 3 guns at J21 b 10.15. J21 a 9.1. J21 d 17.93 I group - 2 guns at J20 b 6.4. J20 b 80.75. H group - 4 guns in JAVA TRENCH - H.Q. at J26 a 4.5. G group - 6 Barrage guns at BODMIN COPSE. H.Q. at J19 d 6.7 Reserve gun - HEDGE ST TUNNELS Coy. H.Q. at HEDGE ST. TUNNELS. The relief was difficult owing to very heavy state of the ground and the long distances to be covered. The awkward cross-relief was successfully carried out. Relief was complete by dawn OCT. 21.	
		OCT 21		[initials]
"	OCT. 22		Enemy shelled BODMIN COPSE throughout the night. Duckboard tracks shelled machine gun fire swept the eastern end of BODMIN COPSE.	[initials]
"	OCT 23		BODMIN COPSE again shelled. Enemy retaliation promptly followed our practice barrage. Vicinity of CANADA TUNNELS shelled with heavies. During night 22/23 Pte COLDHAM when acting as guide to a forward position became missing and was not heard of again.	[initials]

A5834 Wt. W4973/M687 750,000 8/16 D. D. & L. Ltd. Forms/C.2118/13.

Instructions regarding War Diaries and Intelligence Summaries are contained in F. S. Regs., Part II. and the Staff Manual respectively. Title pages will be prepared in manuscript.

WAR DIARY
or
INTELLIGENCE SUMMARY.
(Erase heading not required.)

Army Form C. 2118.

Place	Date	Hour	Summary of Events and Information	Remarks and references to Appendices
SHREWSBURY FOREST SECTOR	NIGHT 23/24		Company was relieved. G group by teams of 66 and 70 M.G. Coys H — 91 Coy I — 20 Coy J — 20 Coy Reserve gun — 20 Coy Relief was difficult being much hampered by bad weather and shelling. 2/Lt WREN F. sustained an injury to the ankle during relief and went into hospital. Coy was housed partly in huts at CONFUSION CORNER and partly at WILLEBEER CAMP.	DB
WILLEBEER CAMP	OCT. 24		Day spent in assembling the Company at WILLEBEER and in cleaning guns and equipment.	DB
"	OCT 25		Cleaning and training parades in camp.	DB
"	OCT 26		Training in Camp. Brigadier General Commanding awarded Military Medals to SGTS KILPATRICK, MALTBY and FARMER on a Company parade.	DB
"	OCT 27 28		} Training in Camp DB	
"	OCT. 29		No. 2 Section under LT. VALENTINE and No. 3 Section under 2/Lt TIBBIT relieved barrage guns of 22nd M.G. Coy No. 2 Section taking over 'A' Battery at J 25 b 4 7 No. 3 — 'B' — J 25 a 6 3 These guns came under the command for tactical purposes of the 228th M.G. Coy Remaining half Coy — training in camp	DB

A5834 Wt. W4973/M687 750,000 8/16 D. D. & L. Ltd. Forms/C.2118/13.

Army Form C. 2118.

WAR DIARY
or
INTELLIGENCE SUMMARY.

(Erase heading not required.)

Instructions regarding War Diaries and Intelligence Summaries are contained in F. S. Regs., Part II. and the Staff Manual respectively. Title pages will be prepared in manuscript.

Place	Date	Hour	Summary of Events and Information	Remarks and references to Appendices
CAMP NEAR BRASSERIE AT N5d. 9.9.	OCT. 30.		Coy moved to this camp from WILLEBEER and spent the day pitching camp constructing dugouts & shelters & in providing protection to tents and shelters against aerial bombs. 20000 rds on pack mules sent up to 'A' Battery.	[illegible]
	OCT. 31		Training in Camp. Ration party transported rations to 'A' & 'B' Batteries.	[illegible]

J. E. H. Whitby Capt.
O.C. 117 M.G. Coy

A5834 Wt. W4973/M687 750,000 8/16 D. D. & L. Ltd. Forms/C.2118/13.

SECRET

Copy No. 8

Operation Order No. 6
by Capt. L. E. H. WHITBY.
commanding 117th Machine Gun Company
15th October, 1917.

Reference Map SHREWSBURY FOREST 1/10,000 and SHEET 28 1/40,000.

1. RELIEF Nos. 1 and 4 Sections in conjunction with 228 Machine Gun Company will relieve the 111th Machine Gun Company on the afternoon of the 16th October.

2. POSITIONS. No. 1 Section will take over barrage positions at J. 25 a 6 3 and will be known as "A" Battery.
No. 4 Section will take over barrage positions at J. 25. b. 3 4 and will be known as "B" Battery.
2nd Lt. ROWLANDS will be in charge of "A" and "B" Batteries and will establish his Headquarters in the vicinity of "A" Battery.

3. COMMAND. For tactical purposes these two Batteries will be under the command of O.C., 228th Machine Gun Company with Headquarters at HEDGE STREET TUNNELS.

4. GUIDES from 111th Company will meet gun teams at I 28 a 9 5 at 3 p.m. (16th of October).

5. TRANSPORT. One limber with eight guns and equipment and four belt boxes per gun will be at I 28 a 9 5 (Junction of TOWSEYS Track and the VERBRANDEN-MOLEN Road at 2.45 p.m. on the 16th inst. Two spare parts boxes per Battery will be taken in; for other guns first aid cases only. Two clinometers per Battery will be taken in, and a good supply of oil.

6. TEAMS will consist of four men per gun, with one Officer and two N.C.O's per Battery in addition. 2nd Lt. McSWAN will be with O.C. Battery.

7. RUNNERS. Two signallers will proceed with the teams and will be used as runners from 228 Company Headquarters to the guns and also from 228 Coy. to 117 Coy Headquarters (N. 9. d 7 5). Two telephones will be taken in by these signallers, and they will report at HEDGE STREET for instructions.

8. RELIEF COMPLETE will be reported to 228 Company and a list of stores taken over, handed in at the same time, to be forwarded to 117th Company Headquarters as soon as it is possible. Tripods and Ten belt boxes per gun will be taken over from the relieved Company. If time does not permit of the trench stores, etc. being checked with the lists, the word "unchecked" should be added to the receipt and a complete check made at the earliest opportunity and a receipt forwarded to the unit concerned.

9. INFORMATION. All possible information at gun positions, and calculations with out-going Officers' signatures to be taken over.

10. LORRIES. Two lorries will be at WILLEBEEK Camp N[illegible] 9 d at 2 p.m. on the 16th to carry personnel to the line.

11. CASUALTIES will be reported to 117 Coy. Headquarters via 228 Coy. Headquarters, daily. This report together with Situation Report and all indents for R.E. material, gun stores to replace any destroyed should reach 117th Company Headquarters by one p.m.

12. TRENCH FEET. Battery Officers will see that every man in their teams has two pairs of serviceable socks in addition to the pair he is wearing. Socks will be changed daily, and feet rubbed with whale oil, under the supervision of an Officer.
If possible, thigh boots should be taken over and a receipt forwarded to Company Headquarters with gun store receipt.

13. RATIONS. Twenty four hours rations will be carried in on the man, and one petrol tin of water per team. Rations will be delivered at HEDGE STREET at 3 p.m. daily for the succeeding days. All empty petrol tins will be sent back on the ration limbers.

L.E.H. Whitby. Captn.

O.C., 117th Machine Gun Company.

Copies issued at 9.30 p.m. to
1. O.C., 117th Company
2. O.C., No. 1 Section
3. O.C., No. 4 Section
4. T.O., 117th Company
5. 117th Infantry Brigade Headquarters
6. D.M.G.O.
7. O.C. 228th Company
8. War Diary
10. File

SECRET [illegible] OPERATION ORDER No 7 [illegible] COPY [illegible] 14

CAPT L.E.H. WHITBY

REF: SHEET [illegible] [illegible] and SHREWSBURY FOREST 1/10,000

1. 117 M.G. Coy will relieve 116 M.G. Coy on October [illegible]. Relief to be complete by dawn Oct [illegible]. [illegible] M.G. Coy will relieve the right [illegible] of 117 M.G. [illegible] of 20th Oct.

2. [illegible]: Guns will be distributed as follows:
[illegible] No 2 Sectn under [illegible] [illegible]; [illegible]
[illegible] [illegible]
[illegible] No 3 Sectn under 2/Lt [illegible] at [illegible] [illegible]
[illegible] under 2/Lt [illegible] at [illegible] [illegible]. These guns will [illegible]
[illegible] [illegible] No 3 Sectn
[illegible] [illegible] STREET

3. GUIDES: a. Guides [illegible] group [illegible] 2 guides [illegible] forming party [illegible] and the [illegible] (J.22.a.4.8) [illegible]
b. [illegible] (one from each battery) will be at [illegible]
c. [illegible] M.G. Coy at [illegible] STREET [illegible] guides [illegible] Coy, lead them [illegible] Sectn [illegible]
[illegible] group
[illegible] group

4. PERSONNEL, EQUIPMENT: [illegible] One N.C.O. will be [illegible] one man to act as Runner.
H.Q. will consist of [illegible] consisting of [illegible] per Section. This excludes the [illegible] Section [illegible].
For No 2 and 3 Sectns the following will be taken [illegible] [illegible]
at present with the batteries [illegible] will be taken to their new positions.
[illegible] will collect all [illegible] together with the [illegible] with the Section.
The telephone [illegible] Section will be returned to Coy H.Q. on the afternoon of 20th Oct.

5. H.Q.: Advanced [illegible] STREET [illegible] 20th Oct.
Rear [illegible] (M.4.d) [illegible]

6. STORES: For No 2 and 3 [illegible] and receipts forwarded to [illegible] by dawn [illegible].
For No 1 and 4 Sectns [illegible]
H.Q. by dawn [illegible].

7. COMMUNICATION: will be by runners to Coy H.Q. Sectn Runners will have Coy H.Q. pointed out [illegible] H.Q. [illegible] with each Section [illegible] way [illegible] to Coy H.Q. by dawn [illegible]
[illegible] with No 1 and 2 Sectns will perform this duty for the Sectns.
Telephonic communication [illegible] with [illegible] group if possible.

8. [illegible]: will be reported to Coy H.Q. by code word OK by dawn 21st Oct.

9. REPORTS: The following [illegible]: Casualties, Intelligence and Situation [illegible] and [illegible] to reach [illegible] DAILY [illegible] and Equipment destroyed to reach H.Q. [illegible]
A [illegible] for all [illegible] will be rendered on the attached proforma (Form A [illegible] Form B for [illegible]) by 5 pm [illegible]
[illegible]

10. RATIONS and TRANSPORT: [illegible] will be taken [illegible] at Coy H.Q.
[illegible]
[illegible]

11. [illegible]: [illegible] will be carried [illegible]
and [illegible]

12. [illegible]: [illegible] at the same time.

13. [illegible]: [illegible] 2, 3, H.Q.
[illegible]

14. [illegible]: [illegible] will [illegible] of
No 3 Sectn [illegible]

15. [illegible]: [illegible] 3 days and be relieved by 7th Division. Every [illegible] to prepare the ground for offensive operations, to improve [illegible] dugouts, and take as much [illegible] as possible.

15 b: Particular attention must be paid to forwarding Trench Ret. Group officers will make [illegible] returns with their daily reports that [illegible] have been [illegible] with [illegible]

c: Trench discipline will be strictly maintained [illegible] and [illegible] clear equipment.

16 ACKNOWLEDGE.

Issued at 1.30pm [illegible]

[illegible] Capt
O.C. 117 M.G. Coy

Copy No. 1 O.C. 117 M.G. Coy
— — 2 Lt CROMARTY
— — 3 Lt VALENTINE
— — 4 2/Lt GODLING
— — 5 2/Lt ROWLAND.
— — 6 2/Lt MS SMITH
— — 7 2/Lt SYKES
— — 8 D.M.G.O.
— — 9 H.Q. 117 Infy Bde
— — 10 O.C. 118 M.G. Coy
— — 11 O.C. 116 M.G. Coy
— — 12 O.C. 229 M.G. Coy
— — 13 C.O.M.
— — 14 WAR DIARY
— — 15 FILE.

SECRET

Operation Order No 8 by Captn L.E.H. WHITBY

Copy No 6

Ref Map: Shrewsbury FOREST 1/10,000.

1 Relief: No 3 Section will relieve 228 M.G. Coy at J.25.a.63 on the morning of the 29th inst and will be known as B Battery.
No 2 Section will occupy a Barrage Position at J.25.b.47 and will be known as A Battery.

2 Command: These guns will [illegible] under the command of 228 Coy with HQ at [illegible] and will be connected by telephone.

3 Personnel & Equipt: 3 men per gun team with 2 NCOs per Battery will be taken in. Each Battery will have two runners (one to remain at 228 Coy HQ) and one signaller.
Gun Tripods, 14 Belt Boxes per gun, 2 Spare Part Boxes per Battery, [illegible] oil, [illegible], one spare barrel per gun, two Chronometers per Battery, one telephone per Battery will be taken in.

4 Parade: Breakfast for Nos 2 & 3 Sections (and Carrying Party) will be at 4 am. Parade 5 am; embus at CONFUSION CORNER at 6 am.
Men drawn will be [illegible] Marching Order with packs [illegible] carrying 48 hrs Rations, Iron Rations and Waterproof Sheet. Greatcoats & Haversacks will be left at Q.M. Stores.
Dress for Carrying Party will be [illegible] Order.

5 Carrying Party: C.S.M. will detail a carrying party of 33 men per Battery with a Sergeant in charge of each Battery Party. This party will breakfast at 4 am, and carry to the line for the Sections, [illegible] reporting to the present Camp.

6 Transport: Transport Officer will detail necessary transport to carry gun stuff and water to KNOLL FARM by 7.30 am.
20 Boxes S.A.A. will be taken up to A. Battery on the Evening of the 29th/30th by Pack transport (for guide vide Para 8).

7 Reports: Relief Complete will be reported to O.C. Coy by the Carrying Party on its return and a list of Trench Stores taken over forwarded at the same time.
All further reports, indents etc will be sent to the new Coy Camp at N.5.d.99 (near the BRASSERIE).

8 Guides: 1 A guide for B Battery will be at VERBRANDENMOLEN X Roads at 7 am.
2 Sergt NEVILLE will guide A Battery to its position.
3 O.C. A Battery will arrange for guides to be at KNOLL FARM to guide Pack Train with S.A.A. (vide Para 6).

9 ACKNOWLEDGE

Copy No 1 OC 117 M.G. Coy
No 2 1st Valentines
No 3 21st TIGHT
No 4 HQ 117 Inf Bde
No 5 D.M.G.O.
No 6 WAR DIARY.

L.E.H. Whitby Captn
OC 117 MG Coy

Army Form C. 2118.

WAR DIARY
or
~~INTELLIGENCE SUMMARY~~.
(Erase heading not required.)

Instructions regarding War Diaries and Intelligence Summaries are contained in F. S. Regs., Part II. and the Staff Manual respectively. Title pages will be prepared in manuscript.

117 M.G. Coy

Place	Date	Hour	Summary of Events and Information	Remarks and references to Appendices
YPRES SECTOR	MONTH OF OCTOBER ~~NOVEMBER~~		The Use of Machine Guns for Barrage Work:	KGHW

During the past month there have been a great many Machine Guns used to put down a M.G. Barrage on an S.O.S. line. For this purpose as many as 20 Machine Guns have been employed on a Brigade Front. The efficiency of a Machine Gun Barrage for S.O.S. work is undoubted but it is pointed out that the employment of such a large number of guns throws a great strain on a Brigade Machine Gun Company. It has frequently happened that a Brigade Company has done duty with its own Brigade, has come out of the line, and has almost immediately had to supply eight guns for Barrage work under the Divisional Machine Gun Company. These guns have not been relieved before the Bde has gone in again and have usually been moved from their Barrage position to a forward position when the Brigade has come into the line again. These guns have frequently done twelve or fourteen days in the line with a rest of only 3 days.

There are obvious disadvantages in this system:

(a) Strain.

(b) A Bde Machine Gun Coy Commander has rarely had the whole Coy under his Command.

(c) Responsibility for Bde Guns detailed to work with the Divisional Coy is a matter for argument if anything goes wrong.

It is questionable whether this large number of guns for this kind of work is necessary, and a solution to the difficulty will possibly be found in the following:

(1) Cut down the number of Barrage Guns.

(2) Increase the establishment of a Bde Coy by four guns to enable each Bde Coy to do its own Barrage work and remain consistently with its own Brigade.

This increase to be made at the expense of the Divisional Coy, and make Machine Guns a purely Brigade weapon instead of a Semi-Division, Semi-Brigade weapon.

The idea that the present system of warfare is the normal system seems to predominate. As long as trench warfare prevails the Artillery characteristics of the Vickers gun come greatly to the fore. Before open warfare ~~the Infantry~~ characteristics are the only practicable ones. [illegible] it will be found that Barrage work would only be useful in Rear Guard Actions and in outpost positions. In this case it would seem to be wrong to emphasise the Artillery characteristics to the ~~extent~~ extent of organising Machine Guns for nothing but Artillery work under Divisional Command.

K.G.H. Whitby, Capt.
O.C. 117 M.G. Coy

A5834 Wt. W4973/M687 750,000 8/16 D. D. & L. Ltd. Forms/C.2118/13.

Army Form C. 2118.

Instructions regarding War Diaries and Intelligence Summaries are contained in F. S. Regs., Part II. and the Staff Manual respectively. Title pages will be prepared in manuscript.

WAR DIARY
or
~~INTELLIGENCE~~ SUMMARY.
(Erase heading not required.)

Vol 19

Place	Date	Hour	Summary of Events and Information	Remarks and references to Appendices
			WAR DIARY 117 COY. MACHINE GUN CORPS 1 Nov. — 30 Nov. 1917	

A5834 Wt. W4973/M687 750,000 8/16 D. D. & L. Ltd. Forms/C.2118/13.

Instructions regarding War Diaries and Intelligence Summaries are contained in F. S. Regs., Part II. and the Staff Manual respectively. Title pages will be prepared in manuscript.

WAR DIARY
or
INTELLIGENCE ~~SUMMARY~~.
(Erase heading not required.)

117 M G Coy

Army Form C. 2118.

Place	Date	Hour	Summary of Events and Information	Remarks and references to Appendices
CAMP NEAR BRASSERIE at N5d99	Nov 1		Training programme carried out. Rations sent to A & B. Batteries. LGHW	
	Nov 2		Training programme carried out. 2/Lt Bell admitted to Hospital 2/11/17. LGHW	
	" 3 / Nov 4		Nos 1 and 4 Sections Relieved Nos 2 & 3 in A & B Battery positions. Relief Completed by 8.30 am. 1 O.R. admitted to Hospital. LGHW	
	Nov 5		Reorganisation of Nos 1 and 4 Sections. LGHW	
	Nov 6		Training Programme carried out. Rations sent to 'A & B' Batteries	
	Nov 7		Training Programme Carried out. Preparation for the line. 1 O.R. wounded. LGHW.	
TOWER HAMLETS SECTOR	Nov 8		117 Coy relieved 116 M.G. Coy in the TOWER HAMLETS SECTOR (Operation Order No 10 attached). A Battery with two guns of B Battery proceeded to Barrage positions at BODMIN COPSE J19d 6010. 2 guns of B. Battery proceeded to JAVA TRENCH. No 3 Section relieved 4 guns at J21b 40 25, J21b 40 20, J21a 34 (Two guns) known as MENIN RD GUNS. No 2 Section relieved 4 guns at J21a G0 0 0, J20c 60 20, J20b 80 15, J21c 40 45 known as TOWER HAMLETS Guns. Coy HQs opened at HEDGEST at 3.30 pm. Relief completed without casualties by 9.30 pm. Transport lines WILLEBEEK CAMP N9d 78. (Sheet 28 1/40000). Enemy Artillery active on duckboard tracks during Relief but caused no Casualties.	Ref Map Sheet Shrewsbury Forest 1/10,000
	Nov 9		Enemy Artillery quiet but M.Gs active at night along tracks. C Battery fired 18000 rounds on to the GHELUVELT approaches on information being received that a German relief was in progress. JAVA TRENCH guns engaged 4 enemy aeroplanes. LGHW	
	Nov 10		Artillery Activity Small. JAVA TRENCH shelled with Phosgene from Midnight 10th to 2am (11th).	

A5834 Wt. W4973/M687 750,000 8/16 D. D. & L. Ltd. Forms/C.2118/13.

Army Form C. 2118.

WAR DIARY
or
~~INTELLIGENCE SUMMARY.~~
(*Erase heading not required.*)

Instructions regarding War Diaries and Intelligence Summaries are contained in F. S. Regs., Part II. and the Staff Manual respectively. Title pages will be prepared in manuscript.

117 M G Coy

Place	Date	Hour	Summary of Events and Information	Remarks and references to Appendices
TOWER HAMLETS SECTOR	Nov 11		2 gun positions of No2 Section moved in the early morning from J21a 40.10 to J21d 10.90 and from J28b 70.15 to J20b 6.2. These two guns were relieved by 118 M.G. Coy in this morning. Relief complete by 10.30 am. No3 Section relieved by 118 M.G. Coy. Relief complete without casualties by 8.30 pm. C Battery evacuated its position on new positions being established by 225 M.G. Coy & 118 M.G. Coy. Casualties nil. Evacuation complete by 7.30 pm. Weather exceedingly clear on this day. 5 enemy observation balloons were up directing artillery on to duckboard tracks. Many aeroplanes seen.	[illegible]
do and WILLEBEEK CAMP N9d 75	Nov 12		Remaining four guns of the Coy relieved by 116 M.G. Coy. Relief complete by 6.30 pm. Casualties nil. Coy HQs opened at WILLEBEEK at 11 pm.	[illegible]
CHIPPEWA CAMP	Nov 13		Coy, less transport, moved to CHIPPEWA CAMP arriving at 12 noon.	[illegible]
do	Nov 14		Training Programme Carried out	[illegible]
"	" 15		117 Coy. relieved the 118 Coy. in the POLDERHOEK CHATEAU area with 16 guns. The Coy left CHIPPEWA in motor lorries at 1.30 p.m., they disembussed at SHRAPNEL CORNER at 2.30 pm. proceeded by march route to the junction of PLUMERS DRIVE and 'E' Track via ZILLEBEKE – OBSERVATORY RIDGE RD and PLUMERS DRIVE S.	

A5834 Wt. W4973/M687 750,000 8/16 D. D. & L. Ltd. Forms/C.2118/13.

Instructions regarding War Diaries and Intelligence Summaries are contained in F. S. Regs., Part II. and the Staff Manual respectively. Title pages will be prepared in manuscript.

WAR DIARY
or
~~INTELLIGENCE SUMMARY.~~
(Erase heading not required.)

Army Form C. 2118.

Place	Date	Hour	Summary of Events and Information	Remarks and references to Appendices
STIRLING CASTLE Coy H.Q. J19b35.85	1917 Nov. 15 cont		No. 1 Section took over four Positions in the front line at J16c75.20, J16c75.15, J16c60.00, J22a 80.35 " 2 " " " " Barrage Positions E. of NORTHAMPTON FM. (J15d35,72) " 4 " " " " two positions in the front line J22a5.6, J22a5.3 and two on the MENIN RD. J21b4.1, J21b3.5 No. 3 Section J21d1.9, J20b80.15, J21a85.40 and one gun at Coy. H.Q J19b35.85. Relief was complete by 11.10 p.m., the relief of the front line took some considerable time on account of the very heavy going. Capt WHITBY proceeded on leave, Lieut J.R.A. PLATTS assumed comd.	J.R.A.P.
POLDERHOEK	Nov. 16		Enemy artillery activity showed considerable active. Enemy M.G's very active on tracks from dusk to dawn. Enemy exposed himself very considerably in vicinity of POLDERHOEK CHAU. Many were sniped. A gas shell bombardment of some severity lasted from 11 p.m. to midnight	
SECTOR	" 17		66779 Pte. HOLEYWELL was shot through the head in the front line about 7 a.m. Two guns of No. 2 Section during the night in the front line were interchanged with the two of the same section on the MENIN Rd. The relief of No. 1 section by No. 2 was not found feasible on account of the terrible condition of the ground which had to be passed through. Enemy artillery intermittently active throughout the period. Enemy M.G. on tracks very considerable. Enemy continued to expose himself. Considerable sniping.	J.R.A.P.
	" 18		The guns from J22a5.6 & J22a80.35 (front line) were withdrawn during the night and got into position J21a9.9. Enemy artillery active, a slight decrease in Enemy M.G. activity. Enemy put up green lights when he shelled his own line. Fairly frequent	J.R.A.P.

Army Form C. 2118.

WAR DIARY
or
~~INTELLIGENCE~~ SUMMARY.

(Erase heading not required.)

Instructions regarding War Diaries and Intelligence Summaries are contained in F. S. Regs., Part II. and the Staff Manual respectively. Title pages will be prepared in manuscript.

Place	Date	Hour	Summary of Events and Information	Remarks and references to Appendices
POLDERHOEK SECTOR	1917 Nov. 19		Usual enemy activity. The 118 Coy. relieved the 117 Coy. arriving at STIRLING CASTLE about 4.20 p.m. Notwithstanding difficulties of relief due to M.G. fire and condition of the ground, relief was complete by 9.10 p.m. The Coy. embussed at SHRAPNEL CORNER and proceeded to CHIPPEWA CAMP. Pte. GILBERT was killed by M.G. fire in the morning on 'E' Track, although outgoing teams encountered fairly heavy M.G. fire on the duckboard tracks only one man was wounded. Two cases of Trench Feet	Map SHEET 28. JWP
CHIPPEWA CAMP (Less Transport at WILLEBEKE)	Nov. 20		Reorganisation and cleaning of gun kit etc. Considerable sick wastage. 16 men fwd. daily fatigue attached for duty	JWP
	21		" " " " " " 2nd Lieut. FANTHORPE sick to hospital joined 14th unit.	JWP
"	22		Overhauling and Filling Belts. Pay - Baths etc. Preparations for relieving 118 Coy on following day.	JWP
"	23		All arrangements made for relief of 118 Coy. in the line. These were suspended. Orders received the unit was to move on the morrow to the WATOU - STEENVOORDE Area. One officer despatched for billetting.	Map Sheet 27. JWP

A5834 Wt. W4973/M687 750,000 8/16 D. D. & L. Ltd. Forms/C.2118/13.

Army Form C. 2118.

Instructions regarding War Diaries and Intelligence Summaries are contained in F. S. Regs., Part II. and the Staff Manual respectively. Title pages will be prepared in manuscript.

WAR DIARY

or

~~INTELLIGENCE SUMMARY.~~

(Erase heading not required.)

Place	Date	Hour	Summary of Events and Information	Remarks and references to Appendices
CHIPPEWA CAMP (less Transport at WILLEBEEK)	1917 Nov. 24		Coy. marched out of the Camp at 7.20 a.m. and proceeded by march route to OUDERDOM STN. 'D' where they entrained. Train left at 9.30 a.m. arriving at ABEELE Stn. at 10.25 a.m. Proceeding from there by march route to MAXIM CAMP (L 13 d 3.3) arriving at 11.15 a.m. Transport left WILLEBEEK under arrangements made by the B.T.O. arriving in Camp at 12.30 p.m.	Ref Map Sheet 27 JRAP
MAXIM CAMP (L13 d 3.3.)	" 25		Church Parades — Cleaning of Equipment.	JRAP
do.	" 26		Overhauling Belts, Gun Kit.	JRAP
do.	" 27		Training in Vicinity of Camp	JRAP
do	" 28		" " " " "	JRAP
do	" 29		" " " " "	JRAP
do	" 30		" " " " "	

J.R.C. Pete[illegible] Lt.
A/O.C. 17 Coy M.G.C.

A5834 Wt. W4973 M687 750,000 8/16 D. D. & L. Ltd. Forms/C.2118/13.

Secret Operation Order No 11 by Capt L.R.H. WHITBY Copy No 5

Ref: TRENCH MAPS: POLDERHOEK SECTOR

1. Relief: 117 MG Coy will relieve 118 MG Coy on the night of the 15/16

2. Disposition: Guns will be disposed as follows:

No 1 Section in relief of Lt RUTTER will occupy positions at J16c7520, J16c7515, J16c6000, J22a8035 which will be known as A, B, C, D positions

No 2 Section with one gun of No 3 Section will occupy Barrage positions at NORTHAMPTON FARM in relief of Lt MOODIE.

No 4 Section with two guns in relief of Lt TIMLIN at J22a56, J22a53 which will be known as E & F under 2/Lt McSwann with HQ at J22a55

Three guns at J21b41, J21b35 (to be known as G & H) under 2/Lt Tight.

No 3 Section: 2 guns under 2/Lt Gowling at J21d19, J20b [illegible] (to be known as I & L). in relief of 2/Lt PRATT.

One gun detailed for barrage & attached No 2 Section

One gun at J21a8540 (K) under 2/Lt TIGHT.

2/Lt TIGHT with his 3 guns will relieve 2/Lt HALL.

3. Guides: at the Junction of PLUMERS DRIVE and 20 Bde Track at 3.30pm. All teams will have tickets with the names of the officers they are relieving and will move off in the following order: A.B.C.D; E&F; G.H.K.I.L; Barrage guns.

Guides for each gun team will be picked up at Coy HQ.

4. Personnel & Equipment: Teams will be 4 men per gun with 2 N.C.O.s per Sectn in addition. HQs will consist of Signalling Cpl, Sgt FARMER; 6 Signallers; 1 Batman; Co Runners

Guns A, B.C. D.E.F. will take in First Aid Cases; Condensers + Tubes; cleaning rods; oil etc and 1 tin of water per team.

Remainder: Guns in addition to the above, with Clinometers for Barrage Guns. Tripods + Belt Boxes will be handed over.

5. HQs will open at STIRLING CASTLE (J19b 3580) at 4pm on the 15th.

6. Communication: C.S.M. will detail one signaller to accompany each group

i.e. 1 for guns A.B.C.D
1 for guns E&F
1 for guns G.H.K.I.L
1 for NORTHAMPTON FARM.

These signallers will proceed with their groups & return with relief complete Report. Other communication, reports etc by the usual Section Runners.

7. Parade & Dress: Coy parade 1.15pm. Embus 1.30pm. Dress: Skeleton Marching Order with packs slung containing 48 hrs Rations, Iron Rations & waterproof sheet.

8. Rations: for the 17th/18th will be delivered at STIRLING CASTLE by 7.30am on the 17th. [illegible] with the current. Sections will send Ration Parties accordingly of about 5 men per Section

8. Detail: Lt Valentine will be at Rear HQs. 2/Lt FANTHORPE i/c Barrage Guns

9. GENERAL: 1. ALL WET GUMBOOTS & SOCKS MUST BE SENT OUT BY RATION PARTIES. GUM BOOTS WILL NOT BE HANDED OVER ON RELIEF.

2. A report of any gas shelling will be submitted with the usual daily reports to facilitate the location of fouled ground.

3. ALL MEN MUST BE INFORMED WHERE COY HQs is situated, and will make their way there if they get lost.

Copy No 1 Officers Mess.
No 2 Lt PLATTS
No 3 117 Inf Bde
No 4 DMGO
No 5 War diary
No 6 FILE.

11.30pm 14/11/17

L.R.H. Whitby Captn
OC 117 MG Coy

Secret Operation Order No 9 by Captn L.E.H. Whitby Copy No 7

1. Relief: No 1 Section will relieve A Battery / No 4 Section " " B " } on the morning of 4th inst. Relief to be complete by 8.30am

2. Equipment: Relieving Guns will take over all guns, ammunn etc and all Information.

3. Strength: Both Batteries will be at the following Strength:

1 Officer. 1 Offr Servt
1 Signaller, 2 Runners [1 with Battery & 1 at HEDGE St]
2 N.C.Os
12 Gunners.

4. Relief Complete will be reported to O.C. 228 Coy and to O.C 117 M.G Coy (by the relieved Sections)

5. Rations: 48 hrs Rations will be carried in on the men.

6. Parade: 5 am. Dress: Skeleton Marching Order with packs slung.
Whale Oil, Gun Oil & Socks will also be carried.

7. Outcoming Sections: must bring out all dirty Socks and as many empty petrol tins as can be salved on the way out.

8. General:
1. Rations for the future will be delivered at HEDGE St at 7.30am.
2. 2/Lt Rowlands will be i/c A Battery 2/Lt Stephens i/c B. Battery.
3. Socks will always be carried out by ration Parties.

Copy No 1: O.C. Coy
No 2 O.C. A Battn
No 3 O.C. B Battn
No 4 O.C. No 1 Sectn
No 5 O.C. No 4 Sectn
No 6 O.C. 228 M.G. Coy
No 7 War Diary
No 8 File

12 noon 3/11/17

L.E.H. Whitby Captn
O.C. 117 M.G. Coy

Copy Nº 10

Secret

Operation Order Nº [illegible] 117 [illegible] Firing [illegible]

1 [illegible] 117 M.G. Coy will relieve 116 M.G. Coy on the morning of 19th November [illegible]

2 Dispositions. Nº 3 Section [illegible] will occupy gun positions at J 3? [illegible] (Nº 1 gun) J 2? [illegible] (Nº 2 gun) [illegible] (Nº [illegible] gun) with Section H.Q. at J 21 a [illegible]
Nº 2 Section [illegible] will occupy gun positions at J 21 c [illegible] (Nº 3 gun) J 2? c [illegible] (Nº [illegible] gun) J 20 [illegible] (Nº [illegible] gun)
One gun will be [illegible] J 21 c 40.0? (Nº 5 gun) [illegible] on the morning of the 9th. The Nº 2 Section will [illegible]
Nº 1 Section will be [illegible] A Battery [illegible] 116 M.G. Coy [illegible] B Battery Position [illegible]
Nº 4 Section [illegible] 116 M.G. Coy [illegible] under 2/Lt STEPHENS. The other two guns of this Section will [illegible] as detailed for Nº 1 Section.

3 Guides. Guides for Nºs 2 and 3 Sections will be on the [illegible] road by CANADA [illegible] at 4 [illegible]
2/Lts SCHWABE and STEPHENS will arrange for their own guides with their [illegible] 116 M.G. Coy.

4 [illegible] [illegible] will be taken over from 116 M.G. Coy.
Nºs 2 and 3 Sections will take in [illegible] guns, [illegible] Aid cases, 1 [illegible] [illegible] Luminous [illegible] and Gun Book.
Nºs 1 and 4 Sections will [illegible] their guns [illegible] at the [illegible] positions. All Clinometers will be [illegible] B Battery. [illegible] will be sent to Coy H.Q. [illegible]

5 Headquarters [illegible] will [illegible] HEDGE ST at 7.30 pm 8th Nov.

6 Dress [illegible] Nºs 2 and 3 Sections will parade at 2.30 pm. Dress [illegible]

7 [illegible] [illegible] 3 [illegible] 2 NCOs per Section [illegible] B Battery [illegible] NCO for the Battery. The remainder will be sent to HEDGE ST [illegible] H.Q. will consist of C.S.M. [illegible] and [illegible] will be at H.Q.

8 [illegible] [illegible] Routine [illegible] (detailed by C.S.M.) [illegible] H.Q. with the 'Relief Complete' report. [illegible] Verified position Report [illegible] TUDOR [illegible] MENIN ROAD to J 15 a 0? 1?

9 [illegible] [illegible] Section [illegible] and QM Stores will move to [illegible] on the morning of the 9th.

10 [illegible] [illegible] will be delivered at HEDGE ST on the morning of the [illegible] 6 AM. Sections will send [illegible]

11 General. a [illegible] Gum Boots [illegible]
b [illegible]
c [illegible] Salvage dump.
d All gun [illegible] 116 M.G. Coy.

[illegible signature]

[illegible]
O.C. 117 M.G. Coy

Copy Nº 1 - [illegible]
Nº 2 - [illegible]
Nº 3 - [illegible]
Nº 4 - [illegible]
Nº 5 - [illegible]
Nº 6 - [illegible]
Nº 7 - [illegible]
Nº 8 - H.Q. 117 Inf. Bde.
Nº 9 - D.M.G.O.
Nº 10 - War Diary
Nº 11 - [illegible]

[illegible] 4 p.m. 7th Nov/17.

Instructions regarding War Diaries and Intelligence Summaries are contained in F. S. Regs., Part II. and the Staff Manual respectively. Title pages will be prepared in manuscript.

WAR DIARY
or
INTELLIGENCE SUMMARY.
(Erase heading not required.)

Army Form C. 2118.

Vol 20

Place	Date	Hour	Summary of Events and Information	Remarks and references to Appendices
			1917 1st Dec — 31st Dec WAR DIARY 117 Coy M.G.C [signature] for O.C 117 Coy M.G.C	

A5834 Wt. W4973/M687 750,000 8/16 D. D. & L. Ltd. Forms/C.2118/13.

Army Form C. 2118.

Instructions regarding War Diaries and Intelligence Summaries are contained in F. S. Regs., Part II. and the Staff Manual respectively. Title pages will be prepared in manuscript.

WAR DIARY
or
INTELLIGENCE SUMMARY.
(Erase heading not required.)

Place	Date	Hour	Summary of Events and Information	Remarks and references to Appendices
MAXIM CAMP (L13 d 3.3)	1917 Dec. 1.		Training in vicinity of Camp. 2nd Lt. Harding joined with 6 Reinforcements from Base.	J.H.P.
"	"		Capt. L.E.A. WHITBY rejoined Coy from leave.	J.H.P.
"	" 2			
"	" 3		Coy employed on striking tents of standard Camps in vicinity of L9 and dumping same under cover in disused Bde. H.Qs. at L9b.	J.H.P.
"	" 4		The Coy moved off at 10 a.m. and moved to billets 1000x S.E. of WATOU (vicinity of K11a and c) arriving at 10.45 a.m. with the eight fighting limbers, remainder of Transport and all animals remained at their previous lines (K14a)	J.H.P. Ref Map Sheet 27
WATOU Billets on WATOU-ABEELE ROAD (K11a and c)	" 5		Coy employed on striking tents of disused Camps No. 1 Area (L9) and dumping same under cover in disused Bde. H.Qs at L9b. Painting of limbers.	J.H.P.
"	" 6		Coy employed as on the 5th.	J.H.P.
"	" 7		Re-checking gun stores, kit etc. Packing limbers and Q.M. Stores preparatory to the Transport moving	J.H.P.
"	8		The Coy Transport moved off at 9 a.m. joining on to the remainder of the Bde Transport on the WATOU-ABEELE RD., head of the column passing K25a 6.9 [?] at 10 a.m. Arrived at MAISON BLANCHE at 4.30 p.m. where the night was spent in billets. Coy Parades during the morning for P.T., Squad Drill etc., Football in the afternoon.	J.H.P. HAZEBROUCK 5A.
"	9		A Lorry loaded with Rations remainder of Q.M. Stores, Blankets etc., proceeded under the C.Q.M.S. to WATTERDAL leaving WATOU at 8.30 a.m. and arriving at WATERDAL at 2.30 p.m. where preparations were made for a meal when the Coy arrived.	J.H.P.

Instructions regarding War Diaries and Intelligence Summaries are contained in F. S. Regs., Part II. and the Staff Manual respectively. Title pages will be prepared in manuscript.

WAR DIARY
or
INTELLIGENCE SUMMARY.
(Erase heading not required.)

Army Form C. 2118.

Place	Date	Hour	Summary of Events and Information	Remarks and references to Appendices
Billets in WATOU-ABEELE RD (K11 a and c)	1917 Dec. 9th	cont.	Coy Paraded for entraining at ABEELE STN., moved off at 10.35 a.m. passing K24 d9.9 at 11.35 a.m. Train left ABEELE STN. at 12.30 p.m., after considerable delays at CAESTRE and WIZERNES arrived at NIELLES-LES-BLEQUIN at 9.15 p.m., where the Coy detrained. Proceeding by march route from NIELLES to WATERDAL arriving there at 10 p.m., they moved into billets. Transport arrived at WATERDAL by road from MAISON BLANCHE at midnight.	Ref. Sheet 27 and HAZEBROUCK 5A. JHP
WATERDAL	" 10		General Cleaning up of kit and limbers.	JHP
"	" 11		Coy Inspection by the O.C. remainder of time devoted to Training and Sports	JHP
"	" 12		Training in vicinity of WATERDAL Inter-section Football Competition.	JHP
"	" 13		" " " Inspection of Transport by C.O.	JHP
"	" 14		Reinforcements 17 O.Rs	JHP
"	" 15		Training in vicinity of WATERDAL. Sgt McCALLEAR accidentally shot during TA.	JHP
"	" 16		Cleaning up preparatory to an Inspection. Voluntary Church Parade.	JHP
"	" 17		Training in vicinity of WATERDAL firing on range. Inter-section Football League	JHP
"	" 18		" " " " "	JHP

A5834 Wt. W4973/M687 750,000 8/16 D. D. & L. Ltd. Forms/C.2118/13.

Army Form C. 2118.

Instructions regarding War Diaries and Intelligence Summaries are contained in F. S. Regs., Part II. and the Staff Manual respectively. Title pages will be prepared in manuscript.

WAR DIARY
or
INTELLIGENCE SUMMARY.
(Erase heading not required.)

Place	Date	Hour	Summary of Events and Information	Remarks and references to Appendices
WATERDAL	1917 Dec. 19		Training in vicinity of WATERDAL. Firing on Range.	JRHP
"	" 20		" " " " "	JRHP
"	" 21		" " " " "	JRHP
"	" 22		" " " " " Inspection By the Brigadier General commanding the Brigade	JRHP
"	" 23		" " " " " " "	
"	" 24		" " " " "	JRHP
"	" 25		" " " " "	JRHP
"	" 26		" " " " "	JRHP
"	" 27		" " " " " Preparations for moving	JRHP Ref Sheet
"	" 28		Transport under 2/Lt SYKES to ST. MOMMELIN leaving WATTERDAL 10 a.m arriving at 7 p.m. — Roads exceedingly difficult	JRHP HAZEBROUCK 5 A
"	" 29		The Coy. left WATTERDAL at 6.50 a.m. arriving at WIZERNES by march route at 11.15 a.m. where they entrained arriving at ST. JEAN STN. at 3.15 p.m. The Company went into huts and tents at IRISH FM. where the night was spent — a few H.V. shells fell in the vicinity between 5 p.m – 8 p.m. — Transport left ST. MOMMELIN at 10 a.m. arrived at ST. JANS TER BIESEN at 2 a.m. Roads exceedingly difficult	and SHEET 28 JRHP
IRISH FM. (C27a 15.50)	" 30		Reconnaissance of the line — 8 Gun Limbers joined the Coy at IRISH FM. at 11 a.m. Preparations made for the line. Remainder Transport arrived at DRANBE CAMP at midday taking over Horse Lines and Q.M.S. Stores from 96 M.G. Coy	JRHP

A5834 Wt. W4973/M687 750,000 8/16 D. D. & L. Ltd. Forms/C.2118/13.

Army Form C. 2118.

Instructions regarding War Diaries and Intelligence Summaries are contained in F. S. Regs., Part II. and the Staff Manual respectively. Title pages will be prepared in manuscript.

WAR DIARY
or
INTELLIGENCE SUMMARY.

(*Erase heading not required.*)

Place	Date	Hour	Summary of Events and Information	Remarks and references to Appendices
IRISH FM.	1917 Dec. 31		Company relieved 14 M.G. Coy in the line with 16 guns as per attached Operation Orders	
			JRCP	
			J.R.A. Platts Lt. for O.C. 117 Coy M.G.C.	

A5834 Wt. W4973/M687 750,000 8/16 D. D. & L. Ltd. Forms/C.2118/13.

SECRET

Operation Order No 14 Copy 5

Ref trench map

1. Relief 11th M.G. Coy will relieve 14th M.G. Coy on morning of 3rd inst

2. Disposition. Guns will be divided into three groups

No 2 section and 2 teams No 1 section	A Group
Nos 3 and 4 sections	B Group
2 teams No 1 Section	C Group

A group will be i/c 2nd Lt LIEBRETTIGHT with H.Q. at KRONPRINZ FARM

B " " " HENDERSON & McSWAN " " " BURNS HOUSE

C " " " HARDING " " " ALBERTA

Locations. A group. 2 guns V 28 b 32, 2 guns V 28 c 98, 2 guns V 27 d 81

B group. 2 guns V 27 b 45, 2 guns V 26 d 62, 2 guns V 26 a 55

2 guns D 2 a 15

C group. 2 guns D 1 c 47

3. Kit and Equipment

For front line guns Guns and First Aid boxes only will be taken } Tripods & Belt Boxes will be taken over

Support " " Spare Part Boxes

B group. 2 Clinometers will be taken

C " 1 Clinometer

All ranks will take in 24 hrs Rations, and 1 tin of Water per Team

Mens dress will be greatcoats and leather jerkins with haversacks on back

ALL WATER BOTTLES must be full

Blankets and packs, etc. will be handed in to Q.M. Stores by 10 a.m.

4. Time, Routes, Guides A group with limbers will parade at 12 noon sharp. PTE HART 14th M.G. Coy will guide section to KANSAS X and thence to KRONPRINZ FARM where guides for each team will be met

B and C group with limbers will parade 12 noon sharp. Signallers of 14th M.G. Coy will guide to GENOA FARM where guides for each team will be met 2nd LT HARDING will take over C group and then report back to Coy H.Q's.

5. H.Q's Advanced H.Q's at ALBERTA will open at 2:30 p.m. Rear H.Q's and transport lines at SIEGE CAMP

H.Q's will consist of 3 Signallers, 2 Servants, C.S.M. 1 Runner from A group. 1 runner from B group. 2 telephones and 1 reel of wire will be taken in

6./

6. Communication. A and B groups will [illegible] [illegible] [illegible] together [illegible] [illegible] [illegible] [illegible] to Coy H.Q.s with [illegible] Complete Report and Runner [illegible] [illegible] as soon as arrangements are complete.
[illegible] Situation Report will reach Coy H.Q.s by 3 p.m. on Jan 1st.
General Report will reach Coy H.Q. by 3 p.m. daily covering period from 2 p.m. to 2 p.m.

7. Personnel. Teams will be 1 N.C.O. 7 3 men. All spare men will proceed to Rear H.Q.s and be used as Ration Carrying Parties.

8. Rations and water will be delivered at [illegible] for A group } at [illegible] daily } [illegible] will be [illegible] [illegible] by Ration Carrying party
[illegible] FARM " B & C
ST [illegible] + ROADS for H.Q.s at 1.30 p.m. daily

One guide will be sent from each group to meet Ration Party on Jan 1st

9. General. (a) Every precaution must be taken to prevent guns freezing. An extra supply of [illegible] [illegible] has been [illegible] in order that oil may be kept liquid. All gun commanders will ensure that this is carried out and that there is always a supply of warm oil.
(b) Trench Feet. Men will change their socks daily and rub their feet and then sprinkle feet and socks with powder. Clean socks and powder will be sent with Rations daily.
(c) Fires. [illegible] [illegible] will be sent to A and B groups [illegible] [illegible] group and H.Q.s. No fires not allowed forward of any of the Station H.Q.s
(d) Transport Officer will send as many Transport men as he considers necessary to [illegible] [illegible] to Ration Dumps

Copy No 1 O.C. 117 M.G. Coy
2 Officers' Mess
3 117 Inf Bde H.Q.
4 D.M.G.O.
5 War Diary
6 File

[signature] Capt
Issued at 5.45 p.m.
30/12/17

Instructions regarding War Diaries and Intelligence Summaries are contained in F. S. Regs., Part II. and the Staff Manual respectively. Title pages will be prepared in manuscript.

WAR DIARY

or

~~INTELLIGENCE SUMMARY.~~

(Erase heading not required.)

Army Form C. 2118.

117 M G Coy

Place	Date	Hour	Summary of Events and Information	Remarks and references to Appendices
WESTROOSEBEKE SECTOR	Jan 1st 1918		Relief of 14th M.G. Coy completed by 8pm on night of 31st ult., without casualties. Enemy's activity in artillery and [illegible] slightly below normal. Weather very cold and all ground and shell holes frozen up. Four guns at [illegible] HOUSES and VACHER FARM fired 4000 Rounds on enemy tracks during the night. Retaliation nil.	[illegible] Ref Trench Map B1 1/10,000
ditto	Jan 2nd		Weather still cold. Very little activity on either side. Enemy shelled KANSAS + and WINCHESTER FARM with light guns at odd intervals. 4000 Rounds fired on harassing targets.	[illegible]
ditto	Jan 3rd		Weather very cold. Much difficulty experienced in keeping guns from freezing even with 10% glycerine solution. Primus cookers were used to warm up guns before stand to in the morning, [illegible] portions was sufficient for [illegible] freezing up. Short shot firing [illegible] whenever possible and the use of primus cookers [illegible] to counteract this. 4000 Rounds fired on harassing targets.	[illegible]
ditto	Jan 4th		Frost still holding. Enemy's activity confined to short shoots on battery areas. 1 case of trench foot occurred from an outpost position. Men were carrying out 4th Army precautions against trench-foot as far as possible [See Appendix]. 4400 Rounds fired.	[illegible]
ditto	Jan 5th		Weather unbroken. Enemy activity normal. 4400 Rounds fired.	[illegible]
ditto	Jan 6th		Weather unbroken. Visibility good and enemy did much registering by balloon observation; several direct hits obtained on ALBERTA SLAB ROAD, and tracks near WINCHESTER FARM. 4000 Rounds fired. 1 O.R. Wounded.	
ditto	Jan 7th		Weather unbroken. Visibility poor. 4000 Rounds fired. Enemy activity below normal.	[illegible]
ditto	Jan 8th		Coy relieved by 118 M G Coy [Relief Orders, vide Appendix 1]. Relief complete by 10pm. Casualties 1 OR Killed, 3 OR wounded, 1 gun put out of action. Coy was unable to catch the train at CORNER COT and was forced to march to SIEGE CAMP	Appendix 1
SIEGE CAMP. (B27a 7.6 Sheet 28)	Jan 9th		arriving about 3am on 9th in a very exhausted condition. Great endurance was shown by the men in carrying out this march after a trying tour in the line.	[illegible]
ditto	Jan 10th		Coy cleaning and reorganising. One case of Trench Foot and four cases of Chilled Feet resulted from tour in the line.	[illegible] Vide Appendix 6

A5834 Wt. W4973/M687 750,000 8/16 D. D. & L. Ltd. Forms/C.2118/13.

Instructions regarding War Diaries and Intelligence Summaries are contained in F. S. Regs., Part II. and the Staff Manual respectively. Title pages will be prepared in manuscript.

WAR DIARY
or
~~INTELLIGENCE SUMMARY.~~
(Erase heading not required.)

Army Form C. 2118.

117 M.G. Coy

Place	Date	Hour	Summary of Events and Information	Remarks and references to Appendices
SIEGE CAMP [B27a 7.6 Sheet 28]	Jan 11th		Training Programme carried out. One case of Trench Foot. Snow fell and weather became colder after a short thaw.	[illegible initials]
	Jan 12th		Training.	
	Jan 13th		Training.	
	Jan 14th		Training.	
	Jan 15th		Training. Transport lines moved to C19d62 [Sheet 28 1/40,000]. Heavy Rainfall during night of 15th/16th.	
	Jan 16th		Coy moved into Support in the Canal Bank. [C25 a 95.50]. No 3 Section relieved a Section of the 110th M.G. Coy in the Corps line. Great difficulty was experienced in getting dugout accommodation in the CANAL BANK owing to heavy rain during the night causing the Canal to flood dugouts on the [illegible] Bank. Relief accomplished without casualties.	Vide. Appendix 2
	Jan 17th		Coy spent the day pumping out water logged dugouts and repairing damage done by the flood. Reserve Barrage Positions at CORNER COT reconnoitred (St JULIEN 1/10,000) with a view to building platforms.	[illegible initials]
	Jan 18th		New Transport lines at C19d62 improved, Shrapnel protection constructed and a Road made.	
	Jan 19th		Working Party constructed Ammunition Shelters for 100,000 rounds at CORNER COT and placed Ammunition there. CANAL BANK shelled with H.V.	
	Jan 20th		Working Party constructed six wooden platforms for Barrage Guns at CORNER COT. Preparations for move into Reserve Completed.	
ROAD CAMP [F25c Sheet 27]	Jan 21st		Coy moved into CORPS RESERVE in the WATOU AREA – Location ROAD CAMP F25c ref Sheet 27 1/40,000. Transport moved by road; the Coy less No 3 Section by 10 am train from St JEAN Station detraining at RYLHOEK and marching to ROAD CAMP. No 3 Section on relieved by 241 M.G. Coy without casualties, travelled by train from St JEAN. Move completed by 2 pm. Advanced billeting party sent to MERRICOURT L'ABBÉ [Ref AMIENS 1/100,000].	Vide. Appendix 3 Appendix 4. [illegible initials]
	Jan 22nd		Cleaning and Reorganisation. Packing of limbers and reduction of surplus stores in view of move to the SOMME.	
	Jan 23rd		Training and cleaning up.	
	Jan 24th		Coy and TRANSPORT entrained at PROVEN Station and moved at 10 am. Arrived at MERRICOURT L'ABBÉ at 8.30 pm. 2 Perch poles broken in unloading transport by a limber falling on to the rails. Coy and Transport marched to Billets at SUZANNE (AMIENS 1/100,000) arriving at 3.30 am.	Vide Appendix 5 [illegible initials]
SUZANNE [AMIENS 1/100,000]	Jan 25th		Mens feet in fair condition but it was found that the Anti Trench Foot treatment had a softening effect on the feet and rendered them very liable to blisters on a long march.	

A5834 Wt. W4973/M687 750,000 8/16 D. D. & L. Ltd. Forms/C.2118/13.

Instructions regarding War Diaries and Intelligence Summaries are contained in F. S. Regs., Part II. and the Staff Manual respectively. Title pages will be prepared in manuscript.

WAR DIARY
or
~~INTELLIGENCE SUMMARY.~~
(Erase heading not required.)

Army Form C. 2118.

Place	Date	Hour	Summary of Events and Information	Remarks and references to Appendices
SUZANNE [AMIENS 1/100,000]	Jan 26		Training Programme started.	
	Jan 27		Training Programme Carried Out. VILLERS-GUISLAIN Sector reconnoitred. Weather Misty.	[illegible]
	Jan 28		Training programme and preparation for Move to MOISLAINS. Weather warm.	Appendix 8
MOISLAINS [AMIENS 1/100,000]	Jan 29		Coy entrained at PLATEAU STATION at 9.15am. Detrained PERONNE and marched to MOISLAINS. Transport proceeded by road. Route MARICOURT - CLERY - ALLAINES-LE-HAUT arriving 2pm. Transport much impeded on the way by other Transports in front.	[illegible]
FINS [VALENCIENNES 1/100,000]	Jan 30		Coy entrained at MOISLAINS and proceeded by Light Railway to FINS and billetted the night. Transport proceeded via NURLU and experienced much difficulty owing to mud on the MOISLAINS - NURLU Road. Line reconnoitred. Weather very Clear.	Appendix 9
VILLERS-GUISLAIN SECTOR. [R/57 C SE 1/20000]	Jan 31		In the early hours of the morning enemy bombing machines very active. One aerial torpedo exploded in the Camp (QUARRY CAMP, FINS) wrecking one hut and causing casualties to 4 Sergeants. 1 Killed, 3 seriously wounded. 3 Sections relieved the 63rd M.G. Coy in the VILLERS-GUISLAIN SECTOR leaving FINS in the early part of the afternoon. The remaining section moved from FINS to HEUDECOURT, EASTBOURNE CAMP where they were accommodated for the night by 64 M.G. Coy. [illegible]	Appendix 10 [illegible]

J H Platt Lt
for O.C. 117 Coy. M.G.C.

Instructions regarding War Diaries and Intelligence Summaries are contained in F. S. Regs., Part II. and the Staff Manual respectively. Title pages will be prepared in manuscript.

WAR DIARY
or
~~INTELLIGENCE SUMMARY.~~
(Erase heading not required.)

APPENDIX 6

117 M.G. Coy

Army Form C. 2118.

Place	Date	Hour	Summary of Events and Information	Remarks and references to Appendices
	Jan 4 1918		TRENCH FOOT: The 4th Army System for preventing trench foot was carried out by the Unit before and during its tour in the WESTROOSEBEKE SECTOR from Dec 31/Jan 1 to Jan 8/9. Great difficulty was experienced in getting [illegible] of forward guns to carry out what is considered to be the most important part of the System. They were [illegible] compelled to rub their feet and apply the powder without previously washing them. It is suggested that the 4th Army System should be used out of the line and where possible in the line; but that where it is impossible to obtain hot water, such as in the front line Posts, the Whale Oil system should be used. [illegible] Capt. OC 117 M.G. Coy	

A5834 Wt. W4973/M687 750,000 8/16 D. D. & L. Ltd. Forms/C.2118/13.

Instructions regarding War Diaries and Intelligence Summaries are contained in F. S. Regs., Part II. and the Staff Manual respectively. Title pages will be prepared in manuscript.

ORIGINAL

WAR DIARY
or
~~INTELLIGENCE SUMMARY.~~
(Erase heading not required.)

117 M.G. Coy.

Army Form C. 2118.

Vol 2

Place	Date	Hour	Summary of Events and Information	Remarks and references to Appendices
VILLERS GUISLAN SECTOR. Ref Map. 57c 1/20,000 and VILLERS GUISLAN 1/10,000.	Feb 1st 1918	–	Weather fine but visibility poor owing to mist. The Defence Scheme of the Sector reviewed and found to be weak in the following points. Two guns were sited with only a field of fire of 120°. These were moved forward and new positions sited. Trenches and emplacements were badly in need of repair and Regular working programmes were evolved. Rear HQs established at HEUDICOURT. Shelling and general activity of the Enemy very little.	[illegible]
	Feb 2nd		Weather as on the previous day. VAUCELETTE FARM and CHAPEL CROSSING shelled.	[illegible]
	Feb 3rd		Weather fine and visibility better. Enemy movement noted at X20b, apparently working on a tunnel. Artillery activity above normal and very active in the vicinity of GOUZEAUCOURT	[illegible]
"	Feb 4th		A little Rain, visibility poor. Slight shelling of VAUCELETTE FARM. Inter Section Relief carried out in accordance with O.O. No 17. Casualties Nil. 2/Lt W.A. NEWMAN joined Coy from Base & posted.	Appendix 1
"	Feb 5th		Rain in the morning and mud beginning to get very bad. A new emplacement at X1c 25 completed and much revetting finished. 2/Lt C. ROWLAND took over 2/c on Lt J.R.A. PLATTS being admitted into Hospital	[illegible]
"	Feb 6th		Weather Clearer. Slight shelling of VAUCELETTE FARM and CHAPEL HILL. Two new alternative ~~[illegible]~~ emplacements finished at W18b 24 & W18d 74. Defence Scheme Orders re Reserve guns issued.	[illegible] Appendix 2
"	Feb 7th		Enemy activity slight. Movement observed at X20b and X17a. Machine Gun Active from BEET FACTORY (X14a) at night.	[illegible]
"	Feb 8th		Visibility good and much aerial activity necessitating cessation of work on our positions. VAUCELETTE Farm and CHAPEL HILL shelled; also a few rounds fired into HEUDICOURT. Inter Section Relief accomplished without Casualties.	[illegible]
"	Feb 9th		Visibility poor. No movement observed. Little shelling. Work carried on.	[illegible]
"	Feb 10		ditto. ditto ditto. One tunnelled dugout at X7.15 completed	[illegible]

A5834 Wt. W4973/M687 750,000 8/16 D. D. & L. Ltd. Forms/C.2118/13.

Army Form C. 2118.

WAR DIARY
or
~~INTELLIGENCE SUMMARY.~~

(Erase heading not required.)

Instructions regarding War Diaries and Intelligence Summaries are contained in F. S. Regs., Part II. and the Staff Manual respectively. Title pages will be prepared in manuscript.

117 M. G. Coy

Place	Date	Hour	Summary of Events and Information	Remarks and references to Appendices
VILLERS GUISLAN SECTOR	Feb 11		A new scheme for BATTLE TARGETS at NIGHT formulated and arranged so that DIRECT FIRE GUNS should fire on defensive lines in the event of an SOS call by night. Targets arranged so that direct and indirect Guns cover the whole front by night. Shelling slight. Visibility poor. Meteorological [illegible] [illegible] started.	[illegible] → Appendix 3
	Feb 12		Visibility poor. Shelling normal. M.G activity slight. Shelling heavy in the vicinity of GOUZEACOURT. Later Section relief accomplished without casualties.	[illegible]
Ref Maps 57C 1/20,000	Feb 13		Visibility poor. Movement observed at X20b. Much revetting and improvement accomplished	[illegible]
VILLERS GUISLAN 1/10,000.	Feb 14		Visibility poor. Wiring of [illegible] ground in the vicinity of W24a commenced by a [illegible] under the R.E. Shelling almost nil.	[illegible]
	Feb 15.		Wiring continued. Much salvage collected. Shelling very little. Visibility poor.	[illegible]
	Feb 16		Visibility very good favouring all work. Arrangements made for the construction of two "[illegible]" dugouts at X13c90 and X19a96. Movement observed at X20b, X2d, X9a. Aerial activity great and many balloons up. Bombs dropped on HEUDECOURT and FINS at night.	[illegible]
	Feb 17		Visibility again good. No work possible. Aerial & artillery activity great. Many balloons and E.A^s up. VAUCELETTE FARM, CHAPEL HILL, RAILTON received much attention from shells. Front strengthened by 3 M.G^s from 197 M.G. Coy: 1 gun at W17c72, 2 guns near W23b50.	[illegible]
	Feb 18		Visibility good. Artillery activity above normal. Areas shelled W24c, VAUCELETTE FARM. Aerial activity on both sides. No work possible in forward area owing to enemy balloons.	[illegible] Appendix 4.
	Feb 19		Visibility good. Artillery active on VAUCELETTE FARM. Aerial activity of both sides. The Coy instituted a Pioneer Section of 12 OR^s and 1 NCO. OR^s were found from specialist men and Officer's Servants. Great activity in the right sector at 5am. One of our planes brought down in enemy lines at 4 15 pm	[illegible]

A5834 Wt. W4973/M687 750,000 8/16 D. D. & L. Ltd. Forms/C.2118/13.

Instructions regarding War Diaries and Intelligence Summaries are contained in F. S. Regs., Part II. and the Staff Manual respectively. Title pages will be prepared in manuscript.

WAR DIARY
or
INTELLIGENCE SUMMARY.

(Erase heading not required.)

Army Form C. 2118.

Place	Date	Hour	Summary of Events and Information	Remarks and references to Appendices
~~[illegible]~~	Feb 20		Visibility Poor. Very little Artillery activity; VAUCELETTE FARM and CHAPEL HILL slightly shelled. [illegible] Section Relief accomplished without casualties.	[illegible]
VILLERS GUISLAIN SECTOR. Ref 57c/20,000 and VILLERS GUISLAIN 1/10,000	Feb 21.		SOS Signal sent up on Bde front at 5am. Our M.G's opened fire on SOS lines and fired 20,000 rounds. At 5.30am situation became normal. Rest of day quiet, visibility good. [illegible] [illegible] emplacement at W23a 05 60 completed.	[illegible]
	Feb 22		Our artillery bombarded enemy trenches for 5 minutes at 5.40 am. No great counter bombardment occurred. Weather cloudy with slight rain. Visibility Poor. Good work accomplished the [illegible] Section. Shelling of VAUCELLETTE FARM with 4.2 calibre 10 – 11.30 am.	[illegible]
	Feb 23		Night very quiet. Visibility poor. Day quiet, a little shelling of VAUCELLETTE FARM. Much movement observed on the part of the enemy, also lamp signalling.	[illegible]
VILLERS GUISLAIN 1/10000 × SOREL-LE-GRAND 57c SE 3	Feb 24		Vaucellette FARM slightly shelled during day. A few gas shells on road at W 24 b 9 7. Visibility Good. Construction of emplacement at W 21 b 20. 48. 2/Lt C. ROWLAND took over O.C. Company – Captn ~~[illegible]~~ Whitley on leave. 2nd Lt GOULDING took over 2 i/c.	CR
VILLERS GUISLAIN 1/10000	Feb 25		Visibility Good. Construction of emplacement at W 16 c 45, 95. Machine Gun activity – slight. Night fairly quiet. Our Artillery bombarded enemy front line for 10 minutes at 7 pm.	CR
VILLERS – GUISLAIN 1/10000	Feb 26		Visibility Good. Harrassing fire carried out by L. 11, 6, 18, + 19 on LEITH POST + other centres, prior to the raid on LEITH POST. ARTILLERY fairly quiet on both sides. Aircraft – great activity on both sides. Slight movement observed on the part of the enemy.	CR

A5834 Wt. W4973/M687 750,000 8/16 D. D. & L. Ltd. Forms/C.2118/13.

Army Form C. 2118.

WAR DIARY
or
INTELLIGENCE SUMMARY.
(Erase heading not required.)

Instructions regarding War Diaries and Intelligence Summaries are contained in F. S. Regs., Part II. and the Staff Manual respectively. Title pages will be prepared in manuscript.

Place	Date	Hour	Summary of Events and Information	Remarks and references to Appendices
VILLERS-GUISLAIN 1/10000	Feby 27		Visibility Good. Slight aerial activity. At 6.45 pm a raid was carried out by 11th KRR on enemy strong-point situate at X 14 c central, and known as LEITH POST. M Gs of 48 Coy MGC + this Coy assisted by firing on approaches + strong points in conjunction with Artillery. Slight movement on part of enemy. Introduction of Anti-aircraft Red Phosphorous Stokes shell. Slight shelling during day of VAUCELLETTE FARM.	CR
VILLERS-GUISLAIN 1/10000	Feby 28		Slight aerial activity. Wiring of L9+17 guns. Artillery activity - enemy shelled VAUCELLETTE FARM during the day. Siting of new positions for L 9+17 at W 24 b 38,07.	CR

C Rowland 2 Lt
a/OC 117 MG Coy

A5834 Wt. W4973/M687 750,000 8/16 D. D. & L. Ltd. Forms/C.2118/13.

39TH DIVISION
117TH INFY BDE

117TH TRENCH MORTAR BTY

JLY - AUG 1916

117th Brigade.

39th Div9son

117th BRIGADE LIGHT TRENCH MORTAR BATTERY

J U L Y 1 9 1 6:::

Instructions regarding War Diaries and Intelligence Summaries are contained in F. S. Regs., Part II. and the Staff Manual respectively. Title pages will be prepared in manuscript.

WAR DIARY
or
INTELLIGENCE SUMMARY.
(Erase heading not required.)

Army Form C. 2118.

117 Trench Mortar Battery

Place	Date	Hour	Summary of Events and Information	Remarks and references to Appendices
Festubert	July 1		Barnton Trench heard cry for help, & found an Officer wounded, said he was wounded by Germans (search but could not find them)	
	2		3 rounds fired for registration	
	3		Quiet. Brought up Ammunition	
	4		Quiet	
	5		Quiet	
	6		Building new emplacement	
	7		Quiet	
	8		Fired 24 shots from Island 36, blowing up work in enemys lines. Hostile Aeroplane observed	
	9		Fired 9 Shots from Lonques Rue	
	10		Registered at Rue Oullous & at 30 Island 24 Shots	
	11		after midnight 6 Stokes guns fired 415 rounds. 2 guns put out of action	
	12		Lt Dawson 1 corporal 1 private killed 1 Lce Corp 2 privates wounded	
	13		Quiet	
Richebourg	14		Moved to Richebourg	
	15		Inspected line & chose positions for guns	
	16		Brought up ammunition into front line & arranged targets. Received 2 new guns	

T2134. Wt. W708—776. 500000. 4/15. Sir J. C. & S.

Instructions regarding War Diaries and Intelligence Summaries are contained in F. S. Regs., Part II. and the Staff Manual respectively. Title pages will be prepared in manuscript.

WAR DIARY
or
INTELLIGENCE SUMMARY.
(Erase heading not required.)

Original 39 Army Form C. 2118.

117 Trench Mortar Battery

Vol I

Place	Date	Hour	Summary of Events and Information	Remarks and references to Appendices
Richebourg	July 17		Arranging & carrying ammunition up to line	
"	18		Preparing defence emplacements at 6 points	
"	19		Handed over command to Capt Stevens 16 Notts & Derby	
"	20		Relieved by 116 Bde. Went to Billets at Le Touret	
Le Touret	21		Gun Drill & other training — washing handcarts.	
	22		Registering [illegible] Cambrin — training in billets Ammunition & rifle inspection	
	23		Gas Helmet Parade — men tested in Gas — Church Parade	
	24	5.30pm	Moved to Le Hamel	
Hamel	25		Went to Givenchy preparing to take over.	
	26		Relieved 118th Bde in Givenchy Sector	
Givenchy	27		Carried up Ammunition & selected sites for new emplacements	
	28		Men in Billets attended Divine Service — Improvement of four emplacements by [illegible]	
	29		No 1 Section relieved No 2. Fired 183 rounds in retaliation to enemy's shelling. Replenishing ammn.	
	30		All guns registered on Northern & Southern Craters — fired 162 rounds. Roofing new emplacements.	
	31		Carried up 1000 rds Ammn. Distributed 700. Fired in cooperation with Artillery during Infantry Raid — Expended 700 rounds	

H R Stevens Capt o/c 117 TMB

T2134. Wt. W708—776. 500000. 4/15. Sir J. C. & S.

117th Brigade.

39th Division.

117th BRIGADE LIGHT TRENCH MORTAR BATTERY

AUGUST 1 9 1 6 ::::

Instructions regarding War Diaries and Intelligence Summaries are contained in F. S. Regs., Part II. and the Staff Manual respectively. Title pages will be prepared in manuscript.

WAR DIARY
or
INTELLIGENCE SUMMARY.
(Erase heading not required.)

Army Form C. 2118.

Vol 2

Place	Date	Hour	Summary of Events and Information	Remarks and references to Appendices
Givenchy	1	Early	Mines Enterprise 31/1 7 Guns in action Total rounds of 3" used 707 – No casualties	
	2		Carrying stokes ammunition into the line – Preparing for relief of Sections	
	3		Relief of by No 2 Section of No 1. Rifle grenade activity 231 shells fired	
	4		Short route march & baths No 1 Section Divine Service – No 2 fired 98 rounds. 29641 Pte Brown E. admitted to hospital self inflicted wound	
	5		Quiet day only 70 rounds fired. 390 shells carried to trenches	
	6		Relieved by 116th Brigade – proceeded to Bethune	
	7		Runaway horses stopped by 87 Pte Rumley C.T. 16th R.B's Inspection by G.O.C. Shelling of Bethune – 4 men killed of the Battery	
	8		Quiet day – Spent inspecting the men	
	9		Quiet day	
	10		Moved from Bethune to Auchel	
	11		" " Auchel " Rocourt	
	12		" " Rocourt " Ohlencourt Drill in the afternoon	
	13		Drill etc in morning – afternoon spent in resting	
	14		Commenced training in Monchy-Breton area	
	15		Continued " " " "	
	16		" " " " " "	

T2134. Wt. W708–776. 500000. 4/15. Sir J. C. & S.

Army Form C. 2118.

Instructions regarding War Diaries and Intelligence Summaries are contained in F. S. Regs., Part II. and the Staff Manual respectively. Title pages will be prepared in manuscript.

WAR DIARY
or
INTELLIGENCE SUMMARY.
(Erase heading not required.)

Place	Date	Hour	Summary of Events and Information	Remarks and references to Appendices
August				
17			Continued training in Monchy-Breton Area	
18			" " "	
19			" " "	
20			" " "	
21			" " "	
22				
23			Left Orlencourt & moved to Neuville-au-Cornet	
24			Move from Neuville-au-Cornet to Neuvillette	
25			Neuvillette to Vauchelle-les-Authie	
26			~~[illegible]~~ Remained day in billets	
27			Training for morning — rested remainder of day	
28			Moved from Acheux to Bertrancourt	
29			NCOs visited new trenches.	
30			Gun drill with men — preparing to move to trenches.	
31			Detonating shells for attack.	

H. R. Sleden Capt
O/c 117 T.M.B.

T2134. Wt. W708—776. 500000. 4/15. Sir J. C. & S.

www.ingramcontent.com/pod-product-compliance
Lightning Source LLC
Chambersburg PA
CBHW082011220426
43670CB00014B/2599
* 9 7 8 1 4 7 4 5 2 5 6 1 9 *